ON AIR

THE VISUAL MESSAGES
AND GLOBAL LANGUAGE
OF

ON AIR

PREFACE

Everyone has their own MTV. Over the past quarter of a century, MTV has grown from an inspired new entertainment concept via a revolutionary window on the world of alternative music, visual imagery and culture, into a mythos. Talk to any creative who grew up as part of the 'MTV generation' and they will tell you nostalgic tales of long nights during their formative years spent in the company of a gogglebox in their teenage bedrooms, and about seminal MTV moments of music, art, inspiration and longing.

But MTV has long ceased to be just 'music television'. It is years since it was the simple American link-and-clip cable channel, showing back-to-back rock videos, with VJ hosts and some quirky graphics that sent the 'kids' wild. It has become universal; part of the furniture, part of growing up, part of the fabric of the entertainment-saturated lives of youth. It has gone beyond music; it has colonised genres, communities, regions and languages. It has expanded into a world of reality TV, games, award ceremonies, ring-tones and cartoon series. It has broken free from the confines of the television set and spread to computers and telephones. MTV is 46 channels and 37 websites; it is blogs, games, downloads, streaming, wireless content and, increasingly, interactive. When MTV hosts live events, young people come in their hundreds of thousands and up to a billion people worldwide now have access to the channel.

For 25 years MTV has managed to hold the notoriously fickle attention of teenagers and young adults by continually growing and mutating, and also always remaining constant. It is one of the world's biggest brands, with an extremely powerful identity, yet MTV has found a way to straddle the gap between being huge, mainstream mass-entertainment and having a rebellious, left-field, cool, individual image. How does it do that?

A few years ago, a guy named Herman Vaske went around asking lots of famous artists, filmmakers, musicians, actors and creatives a simple question; 'Why are you creative?' The responses were fascinating enough to end up as a book and a television series spin-off. The key to the success of the project was the choice of interviewees. They were highly talented and fascinating individuals who had made unique and often ground breaking contributions to their fields; creative pioneers if you will.

Asking someone 'Why are you creative?' is as good as asking; 'What makes you tick?', 'How do you do what you do?' or even 'What are you?' If you are asking a person who has produced a particularly rich and fascinating body of work, who is honest and has spent some time thinking about themselves and what they do, then their answers can be illuminating, inspiring and often surprising. If the subject happens to be a multinational corporation rather than an individual, then you would expect the answers to become fractured and dissonant; diluted 'corpspeak'. But MTV is not a normal multinational corporation. MTV is an idea, it is an attitude; it even has a generation named after it. Despite its phenomenal growth, MTV has strayed little from the cutting edge, in its own mind at least, and has made being new, fresh and in the lead – through the patronage of new creative talent – the key to its success.

On Air is a look at how MTV ticks creatively. It talks to almost 100 animators, filmmakers and designers; people who make the graphics, promo films and idents for the channel; the ones who make those crucial 'little pieces of art' that stubbornly remain between all that programming. It looks at a selection of the very best of their recent MTV output internationally, and talks to them about the trials and joys of creating animation shorts for MTV, about the range of technologies at their disposal and how these have facilitated their work, and it asks them about the effect that access to precious MTV airtime has had on their careers.

On Air also talks to some of the people within MTV, the creative directors and producers whose job it is to maintain MTV's left-field identity and prevent it from sliding into the morass of bland uniform commercial entertainment. A bunch of individuals who are often surprisingly rebellious themselves, with strong ideas about their MTV and where its attitudes and duties should lie. It asks about how the channel fosters a continually creative and innovative environment and how it adapts and survives creatively. It asks where the future of music entertainment is heading...and what is the secret of eternal youth.

Sophie Lovell

THE VIEW FROM LEFT FIELD

BRENT HANSEN
INTERVIEW: SOPHIE LOVELL

As President of MTV Networks Europe and President of Creative & Editor in Chief, MTV Networks International, the unconventional New Zealander, Brent Hansen, has one of the most desirable chief executive jobs in the world. How he views and steers the creative progress of this enormous beast entrusted to his care defines, to a considerable extent, the nature of what it delivers to its viewers, and in which directions it will be heading in the near future.

How would you describe MTV's role on an individual level and a global one?

First and foremost, MTV is a brand that people expect to be a stamp of approval for artists and ideas, but it is also a television channel that pushes boundaries creatively where it can.

I think that on an individual level it is like a zone that you go to, to be stimulated, where you will always be asked to have a point of view about something. We put a lot of effort into making sure that we treat our audience as intelligent individuals, not a group, and certainly not a large common denominator. Obviously, when it comes to music, we play the familiar and hits as well as new material, but with MTV you'd always expect it to involve something new or to have some kind of left-field point of view. I think that's crucial for us.

Should MTV be inspirational to its audience?

It is hopefully the most aspirational of all the music channels. That's what I like and I think that is really important. We don't try to preach to people. We don't try to tell people what to do. We like people to make up their own minds; it's more stimulating. Hopefully it is always trying out new, visual creative ideas, to do what so many other people do as well, but to do it better.

How powerful is MTV?

It is pretty powerful as a tool for ideas to be seen. It is where most of the new ideas in various fields get seen first. MTV is really where the ideas tend to start and we are fresh in that regard, but it is music and it is television in this digital space, therefore it is not 'stand alone'. Very little television these days is an event. Once it used to be that even the news at night was an event on television. Now I think we are living in a much more difficult time. I think we do aggre-

gate great network moments, such as the MTV Europe Music Awards, where people pay attention to what we are about. The rest of the time we are kind of like a friend or an acquaintance. You might hate us because you don't like what you are seeing but you'll come back, and you'll come back, and you'll come back because that's where you will see what is about to become successful and what is successful.

How does MTV continually adapt to stay young and fresh?

Well, part of my philosophy is that we are constantly launching new channels and people are being given new opportunities within the system. That allows new people to come in who have been influenced by MTV and have a strong point of view. No matter how tight the system is in terms of how we deliver our channels, there is always a little window of opportunity for any individual to stamp some of their own personality on them; so that's how we keep young. And most of our staff, of course, are within the dynamic demographic range of 18 to 25. A lot of the people who are actually making the programmes, who are actually making the day-to-day decisions, but not the strategic ones necessarily, are pretty much in this age group.

So what happens to your staff when they are over 25?

They become managers, like myself! I'm a lot older than that but I still go to two or three gigs a week and I'm still very involved in stuff; but obviously I'm not going to programme a television channel. My job is to make sure we balance what we do in a more creative way. I think the difficulty in a crowded market like this is that programmers become more conservative. So I see my role and the international creative directors' roles as trying to find new, stimulating and creative ways of doing things. A manager is more about the philosophy and the spirit of the channel and the ones who make it are about the delivery and the relevance.

How do you foster and maintain an anti-establishment and anti-authoritarian image?

We are part of a big American corporation, but since we are successful we are allowed to run our own style pretty much. We still have to deliver the business though. We also have to deliver in a way that makes the channel look pretty together. We are not as edgy and out there as we once were because the world has changed. The world itself is not as edgy and out there as it once was. Eighteen year olds are more conservative, so you've got to reflect that to a certain extent. We also have a different point of view. We are not 'corporate', we are not 'public service', but part of our brand is about having an edge and I've still got to try to keep that alive.

The anomaly is that MTV has a rebellious image but it has become this huge multinational thing; it has become the 'enemy' in a way, hasn't it?

My job is to ensure that there is a spirit of art and attitude within the system.

Is this constant quest to be young new and different a great pressure or burden?

If it was a pressure or a burden, I don't think any of us could be bothered dealing with it. We don't look at it that way. We're just trying to create little victories and I think that's just what you do in life; you have to constantly aspire to change otherwise you might as well just lapse into a coma.

We are all getting away with something in our jobs; that's part of the spirit of the system. So as far as I'm concerned, as long as you feel like you are getting away with it, you've got it half beaten, but if you set up a task force and try to break being fresh and innovative down into its ingredients, I don't think that's ever going to work. It has got to be the individual spirits within the system that are the ones that drive it through.

How does MTV function in real life?

We have a series of channels (not just MTV obviously, we have a number of other channels as well) that are focused on individual markets. They have a staff relevant to the market place, who have a point of view, and they make pretty much most of the day-to-day decisions about what goes on; so they are fairly autonomous in that regard. From a philosophical point of view and from a network point of view, people like myself are involved who create big network moments where everybody locks onto the system. It reminds them and it reminds the audience that they are part of something bigger than their individual business.

How autonomous are the individual channels?

Pretty much. Occasionally we have an event that everyone's a part of; with Live8, for example; we fed pieces around the world. That sort of event gets the full network power and people get to work on something and get a chance to have their work seen beyond their own national boundaries; so that is a big carrot for individuals to feel that they can be influential.

What are MTV's duties as 'parent ersatz' or role model?

Well we certainly don't want to be a parent! We have to be responsible though. We are under a lot of pressure to be responsible, from authorities in each individual country that we broadcast from, not to play fast and loose with the broadcasting laws. But that having been said, we very much try to make each channel an individual that sits alongside the individuals that watch it. We try very hard not to preach at people, but to be somewhat within their zone. We will raise awareness issues though, like sex trafficking and HIV awareness. It's about giving people information through a channel like ours that they may not get through normal means, and we would project it in a different way. Certainly, at times governments have come to us and asked us to say; 'don't do this or don't do that' and we would pretty much refuse to do that. We like to be more neutral; we might bring up the pros and cons, but we would try not to get in a situation where we would be 'in loco parentis'.

Do you think it is important to push the boundaries in countries that are not so liberal?

We try as much as possible to do so. It doesn't always work that way. It is important to make sure that we are on the edge there, and it is important that people see us as a dynamic space where we are trying to achieve things. But we would not be especially anti-establishment or authoritarian either because that seems ridiculous. We are kind of there already, it is just that we have a different approach in that we have a more youthful sense as to what we are about. The most important thing is to tell people to have a point of view, not what that point of view should be.

Where are the danger zones, where do you need to draw the line?

I think that you have to be very careful that where you draw the line is not misconstrued as having a point of view. What we try to say is that sex trafficking, for example, is a big issue and it affects young people within our demographic and within our footprint and you should have a point of view about that, whether you happen to be someone who goes to prostitutes or if you are someone coming to work thinking you have a job and you end up as a prostitute. You've got to be aware of these things and if you are not sure about what's going on, then ask. Make sure you think about it, don't be ignorant, that's the crucial issue.

Do you think that, long term, the core audience will still be found around the television screen in the sitting room?

I think that will always be there, but you need to have a presence in people's lives outside of that. There are other things we can all do in our lives apart from just sit in front of a television. It gives you quality sound, pictures and entertainment, so there is a certain proscenium arch but there is also the mobility, the interactivity and the connectivity that we can provide and we have to be in that space. So we are working on all these areas, like mobile phones, not just to provide a television channel but to provide alerts; more information, ways to connect with a channel, ways of changing your own and I think eventually MTV will be a bespoke service to each individual, based upon their viewing habits.

Do you think that there is a point at which MTV should stop growing?

This is about surviving in the space. We can't be marginalised, so we need scale.

Having other brands like TMF, VIVA, Game One, Paramount Comedy, Nickelodeon, and so on, allows MTV itself to look forward again. We can be more straight ahead on the VIVAs and the TMFs – more instantaneous and more 'pop' – so MTV can be more aspirational, more 'art' and more forward-looking in terms of television ideas. But the idea is not to just keep growing and growing. I mean, I have a business responsibility to deliver, that's what keeps us in a job, but it isn't necessarily what keeps the channel alive. We've done a massive job with regionalising and localising so that we have a relevant point of view without losing the 'international ideal'. But by the same token, it's not just about trying to plant a flag everywhere; we're not some kind of weird empire.

But isn't a large degree of control ok only as long as you have good people at the top with good intentions?

Yes, and that's the risk that you have to take. Some of us have been long-time survivors. I've been working in this company since I left New Zealand 18 years ago. I think it's absolutely crucial to have the right people in the right place; I may have a 'suit' job but that doesn't mean I have a 'suit' style. You have got to hand it to this big American company for valuing somebody like me. I'm not really a businessman, I'm just a music fan from New Zealand who's ended up running this part of the organisation. Most American companies are pretty much control freaks about these things. Some of the people in the USA, like Judy [McGrath, Chairman and CEO of MTV Networks] are very driven by creative experimentation. It's an unusual thing, but it was baked into the brand when it was started, so they will always go for the brand guy over the business guy when it comes to making sure that holistically the channel doesn't lose its way.

DESIGNERAMA
OPENING TITLES

MTV CENTRAL

TANJA ADAMIETZ

ATTITUDE: 'We are creating opinions, not just nice design. My mission is to use my creative abilities to make a difference; to sensitise people. I would like to design a better world, to encourage people to develop a sense of responsibility, to enjoy life and care for one another.'
LOCATION: London, UK
CLIENTS: AOK, Armani, BBC, Campari, Lipton, MTV, Nike, Sony Ericsson, Staying Alive, Warsteiner

MTV HEAD OF ON AIR: Thomas Sabel
DIRECTOR: Tanja Adamietz
MUSIC, SOUND DESIGN: Denis Ducasse

CONCEPT

'This piece is part of the title sequence for Designerama, which is an event to support young fashion designers in Germany. Every month they select a new talent and promote his/her work on MTV Central. Once a year a fashion show is held to celebrate and promote the young designers. The inspiration for this spot came from the fashion designers themselves. I tried to understand how they work, what materials they use and what inspires them. At this time young fashion was influenced by hand-made, patchwork and urban style, which I tried to translate into moving images. The result is based around patterns and collage. Everything is made out of patterns; patterns building up, patterns shaping a city, patterns taking the place of clothes.'

MAKING IT

'The biggest challenge was to find a visual translation for the creative process of the fashion designers. The hand-made animation, the collage style and the playful creation of the city reflect the experimental style of the young labels. The pattern, as a metaphor for fabric, is used as the core element and was designed in Illustrator and animated in After Effects. The city and the catwalk is a combination of Photoshop and Illustrator. All the elements are animated in After Effects. This sequence was designed and animated solely by me. The production process took around four weeks.'

ON AIR

'The feedback was fantastic for this title sequence. Campari loved the sponsorship billboard'.

POGA FOR PONG SHUI

REGION

MTV INDIA

ARTIST

MAYUR TEKCHANDANEY

ATTITUDE: 'Take it as it comes, one project at a time.'
LOCATION: Mumbai, India

CREDITS

MTV VP CREATIVE AND CONTENT:
Cyrus Oshidar
ART DIRECTOR: Mayur Tekchandaney
SCRIPT, VOICEOVER: Cyrus Oshidar
ANIMATION: Vaibhav Kumaresh, Famous
Animation
ONLINE: Prakash Kurup
ILLUSTRATION: Hema Nazareth
SOUND DESIGN: Jiten Solanki

CONCEPT

'This spot was the third in a series of spots about Poga, a character who is a mix of a yoga guru and a pogo stick and who voices his opinion on different issues. This particular spot makes fun of the practice of Feng Shui. In this project I created the backdrops for the claymation and worked on the composition; I also animated and designed the type.'

MAKING IT

'It was quite a simple project to do. The majority of the action was in the claymation, the goal was to keep it quite simple and give the promo some sense of place, a setting somewhere in Asia. The illustrations were inspired by Japanese prints.'

ON AIR

'Most people liked it, they thought it looked nice and the 3D and 2D elements gelled well.'

CONCEPT

'The packaging was a back-to-back block of music. The inspiration came from Indian calendar art and textile labels, as well as from the films of V. Shantaram.'

MAKING IT

'The girl was shot for another promo, which never went on-air. We knew we wanted to create something that was very Indian and kitsch but at the same time contemporary and fresh. We created the backgrounds using collage elements from different sources, from south-east Asian textile prints to Tibetan Thangka prints and then composed them on Smoke with some really basic animation and wipes.'

ON AIR

'The promo was very well received. It was done as part of a redesign exercise so we worked on several other projects at the same time; this one we did last minute because we ran out of money, so we just repackaged some old footage, and funnily it's the most popular of all the promos for the redesign.'

MEMENTO MORI, MTV ART BREAKS

MTV INTERNATIONAL

JOSSIE MALIS

ATTITUDE: 'Having a good time whilst liberating my ghosts.'
LOCATION: Barcelona, Spain
CLIENTS: MTV, Fantastic Film Festival, GRAFF Film Festival, Sobras Film Festival, Elche Independent Film Festival

MTV CREATIVE DIRECTOR: Cristian Jofre
DIRECTOR: Jossie Malis
PRODUCERS: Francisco Javier Maria, Jossie Malis
SOUND: Didac G. Nario, Yadira Reyes, Jossie Malis
VOICES: Jordi Oliveras
DOLLS & PROPS: Nuria Garcia, J. Malis
LIGHTS: Francisco Javier Maria, J. Malis
MUSIC: Augustin Sombras - Belmonde

CONCEPT

'The idea came from my childhood memories of elevator trips. Initially the clip was part of a short film about what happens after death. Later, the opportunity to include part of this short film on MTV arose after the people involved in the Art Breaks selection process saw it.'

MAKING IT

'The film was made using the stop motion technique. The main challenge was to remain patient during the shooting, which took a month, and then for a further month for editing and some digital composing. The equipment included a consumer Mini DV camera, a freeware stop motion program and a G4 Powerbook. What I learned most during the process was related to gravity. In stop motion you need to control all the elements that always want to fall down. I had some assistance in various areas of the production, mostly lighting and animation.'

ON AIR

The feedback was really good. Actually, it's fun to see your work in so many places. Many friends around the world have seen the clip. For people like me it's very important to have a platform to show your work because the main showcase for short films is mostly film festivals. The feedback at festivals is really good too, but the chance to show your work globally is almost impossible.'

POTATOHEAD

MTV NORDIC

MANS SWANBERG/PISTACHIOS,
BJÖRN ATLDAX AND
KARL GRANDIN/VÅR

ATTITUDE: 'Our creative goal is to be able
to look forward to as many of our work-
days as possible. Our mission is to show off
the insides of our brains to other people.'
(Vår)
LOCATION: Stockholm, Sweden

MTV CREATIVE DIRECTOR: Lars Beckung
CONCEPT, ART DIRECTION,
ILLUSTRATION, PHOTOGRAPHY,
ANIMATION: Pistachios and Vår
MUSIC, SOUND: DeLorean

CONCEPT
'These scenarios were originally intended for This
Is Our Music, but the reporters said it didn't fit the
show (and they may have been right), so they were
turned into channel idents instead.'

MAKING IT
'Most of the scenes were each done in a day and
that included building the sets and shooting the
animation. We scavenged low-price junk shops to
find useful materials. We took turns in doing the
animation and pressing the camera button. Some
of the characters would evolve naturally, growing
older and more wrinkly. The pear turned out especially nasty. The spinning Liberace fish was placed
on a turntable, and we moved it one dot for each
frame.'

ON AIR
'Hardly anyone has seen the clip on TV, although
MTV claims they've been airing it like crazy. A
lot of people have been downloading it from our
website though. However, we did win a Silver for
it at the Kolla! Awards. There was a rule about how
many flashes per second were allowed. Also there
was some trouble about the blood, but it was OK
in the late hours.'

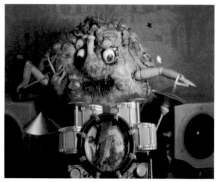

TREIBGUT, MTV ART BREAKS

MTV INTERNATIONAL

RÜDIGER KALTENHÄUSER

ATTITUDE: 'I want to transform an image that is in my head into a film format and thus share it with others. Above all, I want to create visual worlds that have an intensely emotional effect and that have never been seen before in this way. In other words, it is all about wanting to express myself.'
LOCATION: Ludwigsburg, Germany
CLIENTS: MTV, Liga01, Virtual Republic

MTV CREATIVE DIRECTOR: Cristian Jofre
ACTORS: Mareike M. Lindenmeyer, Trude Knoerl
DIRECTOR, VISUAL EFFECTS, IDEA: Ruediger Kaltenhaeuser
PRODUCER: Robin Sturm
DOP: Felix Poplawsky, Armin Fanzen
EDITING: Nathalie Puerzer
MUSIC, SOUND DESIGN: Jonathan Wulfes

CONCEPT

'Treibgut [flotsam] is about being washed-up, and the meaninglessness of the individual in the undertow of a modern civilisation. The concept of a megalopolis, in the form of a strong current, was clear from the beginning. During the development I researched the Internet and in magazines about the enormous revolutions in Asian cities like Beijing or Shanghai, in which entire neighbourhoods are sometimes flattened overnight and rebuilt. Treibgut was originally made as a four-minute student film at the Baden-Württemberg Film Academy. I pitched it for MTV Art Breaks and then cut 15" and 45" versions. The only change I made was to build an MTV logo into the film, which I did by blending it into a concrete wall.'

MAKING IT

'The most time-consuming part was the post-production, especially the photorealist computer animation. The whole film was shot in blue box and the environment created with computer. That meant two days shooting in a studio and around 16 months in post-production for four-minutes worth of film. The whole thing took about 18 months from beginning to end. The new cut and the logo for MTV took about a week. Having a good team for the shoot was vital, and in particular good actors. Because it was a student film there was no big budget, and the actors worked on the project without pay, for which I am very grateful.'

ON AIR

'Of course it is always great when something that you have worked long and hard on gets to be seen by a lot of people. That the MTV Art Breaks project was to be shown worldwide was the main incentive for me to collaborate and the publicity that has

followed has also had a positive effect. The bottom line though is that I did not make the film to make money; and with 18 months production time it would have to bring in a hell of a lot to balance the books. Instead, I got to show people my ideas.'

TITLE

ELVIS CHRIST,
LONG LIVE THE KING

REGION

MTV LATIN AMERICA

ARTIST

BÁRBARA PERDIGUERA,
DARIO ADANTI

ATTITUDE: 'My mission is not to save lives or commit great heroic deeds, it is just a humble contribution to combat boredom and to generate a chemical change that will stimulate the mind and produce laughter, surprise, terror or all of the above at the same time.' (B. Perdiguera)
LOCATION: Madrid, Spain
CLIENTS: Nickelodeon Internacional, BTV (Barcelona televisión), Canal+, Conecta tv (futuravision.2), Swatch

CREDITS

MTV DIRECTOR, ON AIR:
Alejandro Abramovich
DIRECTORS: B. Perdiguera, D. Adanti
SCREENPLAY, EDITOR: Dario Adanti
CHARACTERS: D. Adanti, B. Perdiguera
ILLUSTRATIONS: B. Perdiguera, D. Adanti
VOICES: Dario Adanti
SOUND: Charly Smucler

CONCEPT

B. Perdiguera: 'Elvis Christ is a boy composed of 100% prodigy and carbohydrates. He has the paranormal abilities of Christ and the popularity of Elvis. First of all we created the series concept, the type of humour, the characters, three scripts and storyboards, and then we offered the series to MTV. The idea was that it was to be a series of six chapters, each to last for approximately one minute. It is not part of a greater work although the plan was that it would be part of a half-hour programme. This consisted of a "Zombies of Rock from Hell" talk show, with Elvis Christ as presenter. He would interview Jimi Hendrix, Kurt Cobain, dead drummers like Keith Moon and other iconographic rock characters that are either dead, have disappeared or been kidnapped. It could not, however, be produced.'

D. Adanti: 'Elvis Christ is about the reincarnation of Elvis Presley and Jesus Christ in a single person who creates weird miracles in a little town in the frontier desert. The idea came from Grail Marcus's fantastic book "Death Elvis", which is about Elvis Presley as a cultural obsession. The idea came to me immediately: Elvis and Jesus, both occidental fetishes, with a lot of followers and a big iconographic environment. Were Elvis and Jesus the same person? Why does this character live and work in a little town just on the border between Mexico and the USA? Perhaps because the religion and fetish mix is an important part of Mexican culture. Perhaps it's because I'm a Sam Peckinpah fan, and most of his movies are about the border between two countries, and the divide between past and modern times.'
Elvis Christ is not part of a longer work. It is a series of short pieces, with weird and strange gags, a lot of silences and slow moments and bizarre situa-tions. If you are a B-movie fan like me, then zombies, aliens, evil possessions and that kind of weird stuff are as natural as a morning breakfast. This is the world around Elvis Christ.'

MAKING IT

B. Perdiguera: 'The greatest challenge was using the cut-out technique and at the same time trying to overcome the limitations of the actual animation technique, giving more and more depth of field to the backgrounds, faking perspectives in order to give the illusion of depth. Three episodes took two months to make. We used a 16mm camera and we filmed in stop motion.'

D. Adanti: We made the pieces with cut papers shooting frame by frame with an old Bolex RX4 16mm camera. Then we transferred to digital and made the edit and the sound in post-production. Elvis Christ was a low-budget cartoon series, so I made all the voices and sounds. There were just two of us making Elvis Christ, and we made three episodes at once. This took us two months of work; two months with scissors, papers, spotlights, and our old camera.
When we started shooting the first Elvis Christ we had a problem with the camera. Some frames were overexposed. It was a little tic the camera had. I had to search a lot of Internet forums about Bolex cameras until I found a solution. During this process I learned that mistakes can be an important part of your own style, if you know how use them as part of the work.'

ON AIR

B. Perdiguera: Transmission on MTV means that we got lots of feedback for the series. The result of working for MTV is that our portfolio is richer when we need to ask for loans to make 35mm short films like The Abominable Toaster-Head Man that we made later.'

D. Adanti: 'Elvis Christ had a strong impact on my work. The series was often transmitted on MTV, all around the world, and many short-movie festivals asked me to show Elvis Christ. We had no restrictions whilst making Elvis Christ, which is unusual when you consider that it was made for a Latin American audience where the large majority have a very conservative religious attitude and Catholic background. Elvis Christ has a lot of "incorrect" situations, weird religious references and so on.'

BUNNIES, MTV ART BREAKS

MTV INTERNATIONAL

STUDIO SOI

ATTITUDE: 'Your friendly animation studio.'
LOCATION: Ludwigsburg, Germany
CLIENTS: Deutsche Bahn, Web.de, TBWA Paris, McKinsey & Company, Sparx Paris, MTV International, MTV Asia, ZDF, WDR, SWR, Kinderkanal, Feed Mee

MTV CREATIVE DIRECTOR: Cristian Jofre
PRODUCTION COMPANY: Studio Soi
DIRECTORS: Jakob Schuh, Saschka Unseld
ANIMATION: Torben Meier, Chris Stenner, Carla Heinzel, Elke Herbst, Mathias Schreck, Johannes Weiland, Alan Shamsudin, Klaus Morschheuser, Saschka Unseld, Jakob Schuh
MUSIC: Denis Ducasse

CONCEPT

'Billy Bunny leaves his suburban home. He wants to have a night on the town. So do 392257 other bunnies – Go! With Dean Elliott's whimsical "Lonesome Road" as a defining inspiration, Bunnies was originally commissioned as a commercial and trailer-segment for the Stuttgart International Festival for Animated Film. It was later bought by MTV International to be featured in their Art Breaks project. Visually, as well as in the editing, the piece was left unchanged but got a musical makeover by London's ingenious Denis Ducasse. In 2005 Bunnies was also used as the official opener for that year's edition of Mike Judge and Don Hertzfeldt's "The Animation Show". The original idea of the piece was to meticulously orchestrate a spitfire-ballet of urban traffic to every note in Dean Elliott's wonderful piece. The process was later reversed when it fell upon Denis Ducasse to arrange a new score that was just as tightly enmeshed in every frantic actions. Visually the piece takes a bow to the delirious animation of the 1930s as well as the placid cityscapes of the great Miklos Suba.'

MAKING IT

'In order to achieve the very crisp clean-up for the whole piece, even when shown on the 35mm-film copies, it became clear that, with the given schedule and budget, the tool for this project would have to be the computer. Everyone went to immense lengths to teach that intractable machine all the quirks and flaws of Suba's perspectives, as well as the serious physical deformations characteristic of the rubber hose animations of the 1930s.'

MUSIC FLOWER, MTV ART BREAKS

MTV INTERNATIONAL

KUNIO KATO / ROBOT COMMUNICATIONS INC

ATTITUDE: 'To always reach as far as the time permits.'
LOCATION: Tokyo, Japan
CLIENTS: MTV, NHK Educational

MTV CREATIVE DIRECTOR: Cristian Jofre
DIRECTOR: Kunio Kato
MUSIC: Makoto Yamaguchi

CONCEPT

'We met Peter from MTV when we attended the animation festival at Annecy in France. That is when we heard about the Art Breaks project. The piece was made after being commissioned by MTV. The idea came to me in a sensuous way. The image of flowers and plants and mushrooms explosively growing out of a girl's hair came first and then I worked on unifying the whole tone and image later.'

MAKING IT

'The main challenge was to do the best creative work I could in a limited time. I was given one month to create the piece. First of all, I drew the animation on paper using pencil. Next I added shadows and drew the backgrounds. Then I scanned and coloured it using Adobe Photoshop and did the masking work. After that, I put it together into an animation using Adobe After Effects. An animation artist, Kouhei Morikawa advised me and helped with the movie, masking, and After Effects. I discovered that by keeping the balance between pencil drawing and Photoshop colouring I could build up a new world of soft colour.'

MTV ASIA AWARDS 2003
SHOW PACKAGING

MTV ASIA

ELLIOTT CHAFFER

ATTITUDE: 'Lots of different things inspire me. I love being given a brief and trying to solve it in a way that is challenging for myself, the client and the production company.'
LOCATION: London, UK
CLIENTS: MTV, Channel 4, Channel 5, E4, onedotzero, BBC

MTV DIRECTOR, ON AIR PROMOTIONS, CREATIVE AND CONTENT: Charmaine Choo
DIRECTOR: Elliott Chaffer
ART DIRECTOR: Dominic Fernandez
DOP: Marina Showay

CONCEPT

'I was commissioned by MTV to shoot some live action idents, with the logo in the real world, for the 2003 awards show. I came up with the concept that the logo had gone missing, running AWOL across Asia, and therefore would not be there for the show. The show break bumpers were shots of "Missing Logo" posters in streets, on lampposts and the category bumpers (best female artist, best breakthrough artist etc.) were scenes of the logo with legs in some of the following situations; in a police line up; as a stow-away on a fisherman's boat; getting a tattoo; at the Taj Mahal; on the Great Wall of China; in a Japanese love hotel; bumping into someone taking his 18th-hole putt; getting drunk at a bar and stumbling down the street.'

MAKING IT

'The main challenge was directing people who spoke no English inside an upturned bucket inside an inflatable logo, who could not see or hear anything. We actually had two logos made so one could be used out of doors and another kept clean for the indoor shoots, but inflating them was always a problem. We had to hire a generator and find a local guide at the Great Wall so that he could take it to the top and inflate it for us. Going through customs in India and China was also fun, carrying two buckets with collapsed inflatable logos inside. "What's in the bucket sir?" "A logo!" "Ok go on through." Tying it to a camel's back on the bank of the river overlooking the Taj Mahal was also interesting. Firstly, we had no producer with us and it was our first shoot, but most importantly we had no air and were promised elephants. We gave the logo to some local guy who drove back to a nearby village and got it inflated (God knows how), and then tried to get it onto the back of a camel who

really did not see the funny side of the situation, and kept bolting off with the logo slowly slipping off his back. Moral: Never work with inflatables and camels.'

ON AIR

'There was great feedback from the audience and journalists for the 2003 idents. I went to the awards show and they had these big live text screens and kids kept on texting, wishing the logo good luck on his travels and hoping he was ok! Also in the press the next day, a journalist slagged off Robbie Williams for being too cool for school and said that the real star of the night was the logo!
There were different restrictions across the various Asian countries. For example, the Muslim countries don't want to see too much flesh, the Japanese don't want to see tattoos, etc. The only real restriction was in terms of what each spot was relating to. For example, the kidnapping scene was not allowed to be used for the Best Artist from the Phillipines category as they felt that would be a little bit too close to home!'

MTV ASIA AWARDS 2004 SHOW PACKAGING

MTV ASIA

ELLIOTT CHAFFER

ATTITUDE: 'We should all be working hard towards the end goal and put our hearts, minds and souls into what we are doing.'
LOCATION: London, UK
CLIENTS: MTV, Channel 4, Channel 5, E4, onedotzero, BBC

MTV DIRECTOR, ON AIR PROMOTIONS, CREATIVE AND CONTENT: Charmaine Choo
DIRECTOR: Elliott Chaffer
DOP: Dominic Fernandez

CONCEPT

'This was commissioned by the same client as the 2003 show packaging. This time round the show fell on St. Valentine's day, so they had already come up with the idea of shooting cupids. The actual awards that the artists were going to receive were mini-statues of cupid. I looked at Derek Jarman's film "Sebastiane" and Kubrick's "Full Metal Jacket" and tried to make something that was a marriage of the two, basically a cupid army training camp.'

MAKING IT

'The production was handled by 6th Element in Thailand who did a great job for us. The casting was fantastic, the locations were amazing and it all went really smoothly. We shot in the king's palace and were not really allowed to show that it was the palace so we used a lot of dry ice, much to the be-musement of coachloads of school children who had turned up for a school trip only to find eight cupids in loincloths dancing in a heavenly mist! We also shot in a military training base and the only difficulty was keeping the real soldiers quiet, as they were sniggering loudly while we tried to shoot sync sound in their sleeping quarters.'

ON AIR

'Since I worked there full-time from 1994 until 1998 it was not the first time I worked for MTV, but it was definitely interesting to work for the Asian Market for a change; it brings a whole new per-spective to the job, especially with some of the restrictions they have.'

ENGINE AND FOLK DANCE

MTV EMERGING MARKETS

KJETIL NJOTEN

ATTITUDE: 'The process of making any film can be quite stressful and tiring. But if it's not going to be fun, forget it.'
LOCATION: London, UK
CLIENTS: MTV, Visa, McDonald's, Axa, Channel 4, Oxo, Dog Trust

CREDITS

MTV HEAD OF PROGRAMMING AND PRODUCTION: Tanja Flintoff
DIRECTOR, WRITER: Kjetil Njoten
ART DIRECTOR: Dave Brady
PRODUCER: Shannon Hall
EDITOR: Adam Rudd
PRODUCTION COMPANY:
Stillking, Warsaw
MUSIC: Folk Dance - Africa Bambata

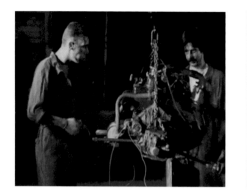

CONCEPT

'Engine was inspired by a cartoon strip called "Ravy Davy", Davy being a seasoned raver who dances to any sound he hears. The idea of using an engine came from childhood trips on my dad's one-cylinder fishing boat. The beat in the film came from a similar engine to that one. To give the film a slightly awkward feel, we cast non-actors in all the roles. Folk Dance was inspired by a Norwegian folk dance that is much the same as the one in the spot, but with more successful kicking and less break-dancing. The idea was to bring the two worlds together and see what happens. The spot works well because MTV allowed us to cut it to any length between 30 and 60 seconds, plus this kind of music is not standard MTV fare. Both spots came about as a result of MTV asking me to come up with a couple of image campaigns. The brief was pretty open but in the case of "Stay with the play", a campaign of five films that both of the spots are part of, they wanted something that showed how MTV brings the world to local territories. From there we developed the idea of showing local people being influenced by things they've seen in music promos on MTV.'

MAKING IT

'The main challenge in making the films was the lack of time and money. I had to film two campaigns, each consisting of five spots, in four days for £40,000 including worldwide artist buyouts for eternity and post-production. As a result each of the spots had to be shot in less than half a day. Throughout the process MTV helped enormously by leaving us to our own devices, from seeing the scripts to the first cut. Also, these spots wouldn't have been what they are without a very experienced and tough producer who knew how to get a lot for very little. Having experienced both big and small budgets since, the definite bonus of not having much money is that this normally gives you more creative freedom.'

ON AIR

'All the feedback I've had has been very positive. Both campaigns were featured in Creative Review, which led to me being represented for commercials in the UK, France and Norway. The clips have been shown by numerous MTV channels, including MTV Nordic, MTV Polska, MTV Spain and MTV Latin America. Engine also earned me a nomination for Best New Director at CFP-Shots competition in Cannes in 2003.'

eternal cycle of the creative impulsive

matt hanson

If MTV stands still it dies. MTV's success lies with courting the individual who wants to express him or herself. To do this, its attitude must be fresh and relevant, aligned to its massive, international youth audience. Like Ourobouros, the mythical serpent that curls around to swallow it's own tail, MTV has to eat itself and undergo a constant state of reinvention if it is to avoid becoming irrelevant, old hat, a past tense; this process gives it an insatiable appetite for new creative blood.

When MTV started in 1981, it was anti-establishment; everything television shouldn't be. Conceived when only a handful of music videos were being produced to showcase artists' recordings, MTV both created and defined a market in those first few years. The visual language it created, the texture of the channel, with its wacky idents and bewildering, graphic-influenced spots, evolved at a blistering pace; and so did the audience.

Many from that audience, growing up as part of the 'MTV generation', have been inspired by the channel's vibrant and diverse visual world to produce their own creative offerings, shaping and redefining new content that will in turn inspire the next generation of contributors. MTV has sustained itself on this virtuous cycle. The evolution of MTV constantly gathers pace, so the channel, now more than ever, is not really about the videos, it is about the experience. As the need to distinguish itself from a host of imitators intensifies, the spots and original content it produces become increasingly significant. No other channel has such a voracious appetite for outsourcing its creativity to a diverse array of new broadcast designers, animators, and filmmakers.

'For us, MTV was a company that we wanted to work with because they have a huge youth audience who are familiar with the language of moving-image and graphics,' asserts Noah Harris, of London-based multi-disciplinary design company, Precursor.

Responsible for MTV projects that include idents for the EMA 2004 (European Music Awards) and the overarching 'Hijack' project (made with online specialists, Hi-Res!), Harris acknowledges that the main draws for working with MTV include a channel audience which allows it to push the boundaries of screen graphics, and the station's willingness to try new content ideas. Harris again; *'MTV seem to give a lot of design firms their first break in television graphics. Of course, this could be down to the fact that MTV tend to give smaller budgets than you would normally expect for the amount of work, so they have to be more creative in searching for hungry designers. But we have always found that working with MTV allows us to explore slightly more left-field ideas, both conceptually and visually. They allow us to experiment during the process of the project rather than having to have absolutely everything locked down before the production process begins.'*

Nurturing this sympathetic production environment has kept the creative field on-side, and happy to share ideas across the MTV network. The fluidity of MTV's identity and programming, the way some spots may only air for a week or so, means that chances can be taken. If mistakes are made and an idea doesn't gel, then it is quickly forgotten. Rather than inflicting lasting damage on the channel, it cements a reputation for risk taking, for letting talent experiment. So well-conceived is this MTV 'house' strategy that only a few chinks exist in an approach that is designed to cultivate creativity.

Net artist-animator, Han Hoogebrugge, highlights one such discrepancy when giving his otherwise highly positive thoughts on working with the channel; *'In my case, it didn't feel like working for a client. There was no fuzz, no long discussions on what I wanted and what they wanted, just a few guidelines on using, or rather not using, explicit sex and violence. And the MTV logo had to be in it somewhere. I proposed my ideas, they said yes right away, and there were no unpleasant surprises along the way, or at the end when I delivered the final animations. The only thing I didn't like was that I wasn't allowed to put my credits on the animations. When MTV shows them they don't tell you who made them.'*

So while MTV is happy to promote the careers of the music artists with their videos on heavy rotation, the visual creators, on whom the station increasingly relies to boost it's edginess amid the slickly produced boy band videos, often get side-lined. Up until recently, this was the accepted quid pro quo for the exposure and relatively high level of freedom offered for a paying gig. But as this graphic inventiveness has come to be one of MTV's major assets in the fight for broadcast differentiation, this has come to be one of the channel's stranger anomalies. It is an irony not lost on the station's strategists, because as MTV nowadays is quick to point out, it is no longer all about the music. And, to be fair, attempts are being made to correct this imbalance. Cracks in its progressive agenda are being papered over. Some MTV channels now highlight the directors of the music videos being played, even programming work by luminaries of the pop video world, such as Michel Gondry, in featured slots. MTV International has a hand in radicalizing and refreshing content across the network, and to a certain degree, addressing this problem. Indeed, this is how Hoogerbrugge, who has won awards for his pioneering web animations, got involved.

'MTV asked me to do an Art Break. It's not a promo, or a station call or anything to directly promote MTV – it's art. Bringing back the Art Breaks into MTV was an idea from MTV International. It was an attempt to make MTV more cutting edge again, like they were when they started. Making an Art Break means a lot of creative freedom to create.'

To an extent, MTV is a victim of its own success. It has moved from being a niche station where it is far easier to be cutting edge and pioneering, not least because what it was doing was new. It has gone from being anti-establishment to being the music-broadcasting establishment. As the ideas and concepts that it trades on have become more integrated within our wider culture, and it has transformed itself into a youth channel with an international presence, it is now partnering with style-leaders and creators who once watched the channel in order to help keep itself relevant and come up with the content for its mass international audience. As a brand, it has moved into a bigger, braver new world, where it is harder to be brash and easier to be bland.

'I think the brand represents youth culture as opposed to music,' elucidates Precursor's Harris. *'It has been cleverly developed to be much more all-encompassing than it ever was before. The ownership of shows like "The Osbournes", "Jackass", "Pimp My Ride", and the huge events that MTV put on around the world, have paved the way for them to become a voice for youth culture, rather than just a bunch of channels that show music videos. At the same time though, what is the brand? It's a multi-national, major-media business making cash. I guess in terms of recognition, it's up there with McDonald's.'*

MTV, like Google with its all-encompassing credo, 'don't be evil', defines the face of the new multi-nationals. The leering clown face of Ronald McDonald is replaced by the smirk of the geek-chic nerd and knowing grin of the street-smart skate kid. Contemporary MTV trades on the new cultural terrain of 'massclusivity', exclusivity for the masses. MTV doesn't have to be on the bleeding edge, otherwise it haemorrhages audiences and advertisers. It really just has to do enough, but what it actually does is more than enough.

'I think it's a goal of MTV,' says Cristián Jofré, Creative Director of MTV International, *'to take something from being underground and allow it to be more mainstream.'*

For all the eternal contradictions between business and art, MTV continues to be an enthusiastic translator and fervent communicator for the underground. It is up to these subterranean cultural movements to stay one step ahead, and up to the visual creators to keep moving forward. In so doing, more young people than ever before get to experience street art, underground culture and the sort of experimental moving images that they may not normally have access to. MTV democratises cool, and as it does so, the artists who work with the broadcast network also get their work seen by more than just a metropolitan, cultural elite.

Music videos can be seen as the interface between experimental moving image, and mainstream filmmaking. They offer a transitory space and the

possibility to play with form. MTV uses the broadcast space around these videos to turbocharge this play; and while it had this space all to itself when it first started, stablemates, such as the U.S. channel Spike TV, also take this ball and run with it. Since MTV first began, other alternate venues have sprung up offering a differentiated viewing experience. This process is mainly due to the digital revolution.

I love my MTV. It has had a defining influence on the way I view and digest images; a nurturer of a scopophiliac tendency I've put to good use. The channel provoked my appetite for the non-conventional in moving image. Early MTV shows like those created by the seminal Mark Pellington and Jon Klein such as 'Buzz', a 13-part series that acted as a high-concept, non-linear bricolage of music and visuals cut and spliced from the global village, had a crucial impact on me and others like me, who would later establish alternate viewing platforms. When I created the onedotzero digital moving image festival, I had in my head something akin to MTV, but without the need to adhere to network scheduling, broadcasting rules and television standards, to musical taste or audience predilection.

So the cultural milieu that MTV cultivated begat festivals like onedotzero and Bitfilm in Europe, and Dfilm, Resfest and Spike and Mike's Festival of Twisted Animation in the USA. The digital revolution has made it just a short hop from this channel narrowcasting to the micro-focused world of Atom and iFilm, online purveyors of video clips for almost every taste. Now, anyone with a website and streaming software can set up their own online channel to show their own work. The way these online and offline showcases have redefined our viewing habits, and refreshed our video forms, harks back to the creation of MTV; it is a similar, but more profound shift in viewing habits and artist empowerment.

Now senior figures at MTV view the online, wireless world as the main competitor for the eyeballs and affections of its natural audience. Kids are more obsessed with their mobile phones than their remote controls. MTV is developing strategies to take advantage of these new digital distribution platforms not only to better engage with these kids, but also to enrich the relationship it has with artists.

Animators such as New York-based PES have exploited the viral nature of the online world to get noticed by agencies and commissioners. The hand-created, rough and spontaneous nature of the stop-motion animation generated by PES is heavily reminiscent of early MTV spots. His visual distinctiveness, and the way he executes strong and humorous ideas with brevity, are the qualities most highly prized by MTV and these new viewing platforms. It is only natural, therefore, that PES, and others who are excelling in these formats, are the creatives being picked up by MTV to cement their audience and reinforce the channel's visual heritage and ground-breaking roots. This is MTV chasing its own tail again.

Recently initiated projects such as 'MTV LOAD' allow those quirky animated shorts by PES to rub up against gonzo street-sport clips, such as 'Wheelbarrow Freestyle', and motion graphic pieces by graphic-influenced directors such as Richard Fenwick. MTV LOAD is conceived as a way to push the channel ethos into the mobile space, and connect more immediately with this new generation of cultural guerrillas.

Peter Moller, who heads up the project at MTV International, views it as having important implications for the Channel's connections between the talent and the viewer.

'MTV LOAD is an ambitious project in many ways. It is one way for us to get back to this creative, impulsive content that has been MTV's hallmark. We can't always get as much of this on the main channel as we'd like to because of commercial needs, but we know we need to take care of the brand, and the attitude. MTV LOAD is a clear shift towards this.'

Moller sifts through alternate content sources to find creative work that breaks down the expectations of corporate programming and broadcast design. This is a neat way to gather content that is geographically more diverse, not necessarily from the creative and metropolitan heartlands of the West. With this project, MTV is fighting the pull towards conservatism that many large, successful companies face. The work that is being acquired and commissioned for the project is making it back on-air in MTV LOAD mini-shows. This is content that was finding it hard to make it to transmission.

'We are also going into the highly commercial and conservative niche of mobile ringtones, and thinking about it on a deeper level. This is an area where really horrible ringtones and animated wallpapers are being sold to kids at ridiculous prices. We want to give the MTV audience a higher level of well-conceived content, and make it free for them; all it costs is the airtime.'

MTV acknowledges that it thrives on diversity, and needs to battle hard to honour a legacy of risk-taking. Creatives and audiences alike may now have transformed into the 'iPod generation', and they still want their MTV – but customised.

The Hijack project is a flagship venture in MTV's efforts to manage the dichotomy between encouraging individuality while building a cohesive, cross-border brand. 'The initial brief was lose and didn't define any boundaries for deliverable elements, it was much more about defining an attitude and trying to sum up what MTV is about,' Precursor's Harris explains. Hijack, in essence, was a toolbox to shape the mindset of all the channels within the MTV network.

'The theory behind it was based on MTV's ownership of youth culture, and the fact that they encompassed so much more than music. We pulled together a huge amount of contemporary, and not so contemporary, cultural references. This notion of hijacking, of taking something that already exists and creating something new from it, just seemed to be perfect for MTV. We incorporated ideas for everything; from bootlegging, pirate radio, stickering, postering, graffiti, customised clothing, and customised cars. Points of reference were taken from "Adbusters" through to the Chapman brothers and Christo. Hijack is also a great word. It is pro-

vocative; especially now we're all paranoid freaks.'

'The great thing about the project was that we wanted what we delivered to be hijacked, to be changed and developed and to evolve over time. The on-air look has been borrowed by a lot of countries, and in each region it looks slightly different. It has absorbed cultural references from those places.'

MTV, as the standard-bearer for many of our contemporary cultural reference points, has been demonised for ills it has little to do with. An unfortunate paradox exists between it being accused of dumbing-down content, of contributing to a homogenous global aesthetic, and the way it positively revels in artistic freedom and thrives on visual sophistication. At least in the content that it has the most control over, channel identity, informational spots and a rising amount of original content, MTV taps into the cultural 'zeitgeist' with an unerringly progressive agenda.

As MTV stands on the new frontiers of a multi-platform world, it is manoeuvring itself so as to capitalise on the creative partnerships it has fostered. Jofre succinctly encapsulates the philosophy that has been the trademark of its most successful periods; 'Copy other people but don't copy you'.

MR PANTS, MTV ART BREAKS

MTV INTERNATIONAL

STUDIO AKA

ATTITUDE: 'Constantly reinventing ourselves, adjusting and responding to the changing needs and expectations of the commercial marketplace.'
LOCATION: London, UK
CLIENTS: BBC, BMW, Orange, Vodafone, Compaq, Eurostar, BT, NatWest, Virgin Radio, Dyson

MTV CREATIVE DIRECTOR: Cristian Jofre
DIRECTOR: Marc Craste
PRODUCER: Sue Goffe
ANIMATOR: Fabienne Rivory
3D TEAM: Andy Staverely, Fabric Altman, Talia Hall
AFTER FX, COMP: Will Eagar
EDITOR: Nic Gill

CONCEPT

'We were approached by MTV to pitch on this job. Various ideas were put forward with Mr Pants being the lucky winner. The brief was to come up with something atmospheric and weird that incorporated the MTV logo. We decided a character was more appealing than a purely abstract piece and cast Mr Pants in the role of the hapless victim of the MTV monster's obsession.'

MAKING IT

'The main challenge was bringing it in on time and within the budget. We managed the first, but I'm sure the studio absorbed the bulk of the costs. It was made using XSI and After Effects. It took five weeks with a small crew to make the two spots.'

ON AIR

'It's always nice to get the chance to explore a less mainstream idea. MTV, to some extent, champion this sort of work and that's always appreciated. To have something as odd as this spot on our showreel is beneficial in as much as it offers a glimpse of animation's potential to be surreal and dark but still appealing.'

EDACRA, LITTLE GIRL SAW MOUTH, MTV ART BREAKS

MTV INTERNATIONAL

DAVID LOBSER

ATTITUDE: 'My ideal work would be one that is both completely original and so obviously true as to seem snatched from a collective dream. Barring that, I would hope that at least my work would stir a sense of aesthetic sympathy.'
LOCATION: Brooklyn, USA
CLIENTS: Nickelodeon, Radical Media, Fuel TV, MTV

MTV CREATIVE DIRECTOR: Cristian Jofre
EDACRA
ANIMATION: David Lobser
VOICES: Nat Jones, Nicole Recchia
MUSIC: John Kessel, Ann Ocalewski
LITTLE GIRL SAW MOUTH
ANIMATION: David Lobser

CONCEPT

Edacra: 'The Edacra piece is a remix of a short film called "Arcade" that I made several years ago in school. I was fortunate enough to be able to spend a year working on this and not much else. The development of the project was very organic; I made a conscious effort to subvert any attempts on my part to resolve problems through narrative or analysis. Instead, I tried to move forward in an intuitive way, making pieces of animation and later finding where they belong. Needless to say this is an extremely inefficient way to produce animation. Six months into the project I threw everything away and started from scratch. In the end I came away with a successful minute and a half of fresh, nutritious animation. Even after several years, when I watch it with new people I can still be inspired by it.'

Little Girl Saw Mouth: 'Of course now, years on, I've learned a lot of tricks and have had many new ideas. So I begged and pleaded to be allowed to produce a new piece for MTV. This one is a case of having some visions burning a hole in my head and finally having an outlet for them. Making art like this is less like tuning a Stradivarius and more like taking a shit. The idea in LGSM is simple and direct, it's a gag really, and not entirely successful. The success I think is in the style, the colour, and the design. I am quite happy to have invented a collage technique that allowed me to produce something so layered and complex in just two weeks. But it doesn't have that subtle, evocative feeling that many of the other MTV clips in this series have. It's important to let things gestate a bit, projects like this need to spend a little time in the womb. Exercises in style or demonstrations of facility are fun and disarming, but the content of a piece should be the by-product of the thought that went into it. There's no way to fake that, extra lines and better shading won't make up for unfinished ideas.'

MAKING IT

'I made Edacra in a day; Arcade, the original, on the other hand took a year. Most of the year was spent thinking and reworking. In Edacra and LGSM I used Photoshop, After Effects, Maya, my camera, and a box of paints. It's important to know what the computer can offer and what's best left to the real world. In both cases I found that making things look small on the computer is easier and more satisfying stylistically (everyone knows the rules don't apply when everything is in miniature). Knowing when, what and how to sample elements from the real world is also very important. Most of the backgrounds for Edacra were shot live with a DV camera and I laid the computer-generated characters on top. The elements for LGSM were also shot live, collaged, and pasted onto 3D objects for animation.'

ON AIR

'My pieces have not been shown in the region in which I live, the USA, but many friends and acquaintances have seen my work all over the world, which is very satisfying. It is difficult and lonely trying to produce animation with no obvious market and no easy outlet. As with most artists, PR is not at the top of my list, so having the support of MTV has been amazing. Hopefully the Art Breaks series signals a return by MTV to creative substance over flashy style.'

LITTLE GIRL SAW MOUTH

TITLE

VENDREDI 21H30, CITOPLASMAS EN MEDIO ACIDO, MTV ART BREAKS

REGION

MTV INTERNATIONAL

ARTIST

DAVID GAUTIER

ATTITUDE: 'In general, everyday life, the observation of gestures, of attitudes, of simple, automatic and banal words are my main source of inspiration.'
LOCATION: Barcelona, Spain
CLIENTS: MTV, CAP Canal, TV3

CREDITS

MTV CREATIVE DIRECTOR: Cristian Jofre
VENDREDI 21H30
REALISED BY: David Gautier
MUSIC: David Gautier
CITOPLASMAS EN MEDIO ACIDO
CO-REALISED BY: David Gautier, Irene Iborra Rizo, Eduard Puertas
PRODUCED BY: 9zéros

CONCEPT

'The Citoplasmas project grew out of a discussion with a friend of mine, Irene Iborra Rizo. She had the idea of making a short film showing a student getting bored to death in a university classroom. Then we wrote a scenario adding a succession of elements and funny adventures that culminates with the transformation of the character. The video clips realised for MTV are all extracts of short films (the originals were 4' for Citoplasmas and 8' for Vendredi 21:30). The Art Break versions were later bought by MTV. I met Peter Moller, the artistic director of the Art Break project, during the film festival in Annecy in 2004, where I was presenting my film Le Hareng Saur (The Red Herring) in the competition.'

MAKING IT

'The short films took several months to make using a numerical video camera, a computer and software.'

ON AIR

'I've had little feedback related to the MTV Art Breaks. It has had no impact on my work. I know these video clips have been broadcast throughout the whole world and a lot of my friends have seen them abroad in places like Austria, Mexico or Peru, but it hasn't been profitable on a financial level. MTV bought my video clips at a low price. The MTV name appears in a good position in my portfolio because the channel is known worldwide and people are easily impressed. The MTV channel is a special client, it uses its celebrity to find creatives who agree to work almost for free...'

ARTIST

DAVID TUCKER, JAMES EYRE,
NEIL MASSEY

ATTITUDE: 'The work is observational with an attention to detail and focuses on both the banal and make-believe, (a unicorn in a shopping centre!).'
LOCATION: Fleet, UK
CLIENTS: Adidas, Creative Review, Virgin, Atlantic Records, Amnesty International, MTV, Island Records

CREDITS

MTV CREATIVE DIRECTOR: Cristian Jofre
DIRECTORS: David Tucker, James Eyre
DOP: Neil Massey
PRODUCTION: Partizan, London
PRODUCER: Johnny Wardle
SOUND: Patrick Rowland
COSTUME DESIGNER: Coralie Sawle
YETI: Ian Charles
DOG: Coco

CONCEPT

'Yeti was originally written as a 10-minute short film for which we shot some tests. These tests were shown to MTV by our production company of the time, Partizan Midi-Minuit. The concept was inspired by the legend of the long-haired yeti, which terrified myself and other children growing up on Arthur C. Clarke's "World of the Paranormal", during the 1970s. We took the environment where this myth originated, and combined it with the modern-day myth of a "perfect" community and lifestyle located in a leafy suburb. The original treatment was to be narrated by a seven-year-old child who talks about a man in the woods near her house who hurts children. She later finds out that dad has a dark secret! We decided to adapt this into a series of four Art Breaks that journey with our yeti from the woods and into the housing estate, each time revealing various human characteristics.'

MAKING IT

'Yeti was shot on a very hot August weekend, something our yeti actor (Ian Charles) was only too aware of. We had made the outfit out of a wet suit so that we could stick loads of human hair all over it without it losing its form. There was also additional padding around the legs and back which made the costume even hotter. We were light on production equipment because we had to move around to a number set ups and avoid attracting too much attention. But a man dressed as a yeti during the school summer holidays obviously meant that we were followed around by gangs of kids on their bikes asking a lot of questions.'

ON AIR

'We had a good response from Yeti and it stuck out from the animated Art Breaks at the time because it was one of only a few that had live action. We didn't edit the series to suit different regions as it was going worldwide and the regions picked what suited them. I heard it was shown on the big screen in Time Square, New York City.'

HERON PEOPLE, MTV ART BREAKS

MTV INTERNATIONAL

GEMMA BURDITT

ATTITUDE: 'To tell stories about the little incidents and banalities of life in a beautiful and atmospheric way.'
LOCATION: London, England
CLIENTS: MTV

MTV CREATIVE DIRECTOR: Cristian Jofre
DIRECTOR: Gemma Burditt
EDITOR: Klaus Heinecke
COMPOSER: Birger Clausen

CONCEPT

'Heron People is a puppet film inspired by the movement of herons, it was animated outdoors to embrace the unpredictable world of nature. The piece was a project at the NFTS (National Film and Television School, UK) in which we had to explore a character in movement. I have always been fascinated by the movement of birds, so I went to the park to observe. I loved the movement of the herons in particular. They remain so static for such a long time and then suddenly move. They are so graceful despite their long, gangly appearance. I then worked with some actors in a workshop to try to translate their movements into a more human form.'

MAKING IT

'I made the entire thing on my own with a mini DV camera. I shot it in June in the hope that this would be the best month to avoid bad weather, but then remembered that I live in England and we never have good weather! There were many problems in shooting the piece because I was filming outside and there were so many elements that I could not control. Some of these elements were nice to work with such as background people, birds and bugs. As I was taking frames about every minute, the people would move faster than the characters, making it seem as if they were in their own time dimension. The light was always changing as well which was nice, especially when the shadows from the trees were moving. However, it was sometimes frustrating when the sun went in and I had to wait for it to come out again so the picture did not flash up and down too much. The wind was the worst element as the puppets would fly about all over the place and become impossible to animate.'

ON AIR

'I am not sure which region it was for, I have not seen it on MTV in Enland, but have heard it was shown in South America. I was quite surprised that the piece was bought by MTV because it is very rough and not particularly well animated. I just wanted to experiment! I saw MTV as big corporation which would only be interested in well-finished work.
I faced no limitations from MTV apart from putting a very subdued logo in the corner. The piece has gone down well and I feel quite encouraged. I am under increasing pressure to create work that is going to appeal to the industry, so it is encouraging that there is still a market for more experimental work.'

ANIMEN PLANET: MONKEY BUSINESS AND MOGDOG, MTV ART BREAKS

MTV INTERNATIONAL

HAN HOOGERBRUGGE

ATTITUDE: 'I was born with the gift of a golden voice, sings Leonard Cohen'.
LOCATION: Rotterdam, the Netherlands
CLIENTS: Diesel, Sony, Mitsubishi, Tros, Virgin, Submarine Channel

MTV CREATIVE DIRECTOR: Cristian Jofre
DIRECTOR: Han Hoogerbrugge
CONCEPT: Han Hoogerbrugge, Jeroen Beltman

CONCEPT

'Early in 2004 I was asked to make the leader for the Holland Animation Film Festival. Together with Jeroen Beltman, I developed the idea of combining my flat 2D animation with some 3D animation. This combination worked very well and we were pleased with the result. Whilst working on the leader I came up with the idea of making a series of animations using the same technique. They were short stories about humans behaving like animals; tales of ordinary madness. I started writing and the Animen Planet series was born. Then my agent in London (Pixelspew, Gerrie Smits) asked if I was interested in doing some animations for MTV Art Breaks. I told him that Animen Planet would be perfect. We made some samples and storyboards and MTV accepted them.'

MAKING IT

'Although Jeroen and I learned a lot while making the Holland Animation Film Festival leader we still had to solve a few problems concerning the combination of 2D and 3D animation. In a nutshell the problem was, how to combine elements with no depth or perspective in an environment that has a lot of depth and perspective. It's like placing cardboard figures in a landscape. If you move around a 2D object with a camera you'll see that it's flat. One of the solutions was to have 2D objects always facing straight into the camera, no matter what movements the camera made. The other problem was texture. Textures in 3D are very rich whilst textures in my 2D animations are simple and flat. Placing one of my 2D animations in a 3D environment made it stand out too much. We solved this problem by adding more 2D elements to the 3D landscape like plants and trees.

As always there wasn't much time. We had to deliver the animations in six weeks so that's how long it took to make them.

ON AIR

'We made the animations for MTV international, which means they were sent to MTV divisions all over the world, leaving it up to them whether to use them. I know they were often shown in South America because people from there mailed me. Otherwise, I have no idea where they were aired. Not in my country, that's for sure. No client is the same. You always have to wait and see how they respond to what you come up with. Working for MTV turned out to be pretty cool. They were very easy, they liked what we came up with, there was no hassle, no second thoughts. There were the usual restrictions: no explicit violence, no explicit sex. The only thing I didn't like was that we were not al-lowed to show credits in the animations so no-one knows who made them. But that's a thing I don't understand about music stations in general; you always get to see the name of the performing artist and the song but never the name of the director of the clip. Having MTV in your portfolio is nice of course and helps in getting other commissions.'

TITLE

TOP 5 INTERACTIVO

REGION

MTV LATIN AMERICA

ARTIST

RAMIRO TORRES

ATTITUDE: 'Creating pieces that communicate the essence of the brand in the most creative possible way.'
LOCATION: Portland, Oregon, USA
CLIENTS: MTV, Nike, MUN2, AXN, VOY

CREDITS

MTV DIRECTOR, ON AIR:
Alejandro Abramovich
ART DIRECTOR: Ricardo de Montreuil
PRODUCER, MOTION GRAPHICS
DESIGNER: Ramiro Torres
3D ANIMATION: Juan Somarriba,
Alex Friderici
SOUND DESIGN: Andres Caceres

CONCEPT

'These pieces were part of the image change for MTV Latin America. The inspiration was urban young culture in Latin America. I shot on location in Mexico Federal District (DF). I used anime characters inspired from the 1970s shows that I watched when I was a kid, as well as the ones I watch now, combined with graffiti, balloons and urban landscape.'

MAKING IT

'Working within a very tight schedule was a challenge since I had to travel to Mexico DF, shoot, edit, animate and composite in a short amount of time. We used an HD camera, digital stills, After Effects, Illustrator, Lightwave and Maya. It was a fun project to work on.'

ON AIR

'The feedback form the audience was great. I think this clip was used in other MTV regions. In this project we wanted to communicate with our audience and inspire them with their own city and in their streets using their language.'

AU ZONE

MTV RUSSIA

ANTON SAKARA

ATTITUDE: 'For me it is vital to create things that find a consumer.'
LOCATION: Moscow, Russia
CLIENTS: 1st State Channel of Russia, Channel Russia, MTV Russia, MTV Central Europe, Fox Italy, McCann Ericsson, Darcy

CREDITS

MTV CREATIVE DIRECTOR: Ilya Bachurin
DESIGN, ANIMATION, SOUND:
Anton Sakara

CONCEPT
'The goal here was to create a graphic spot that represented Russian music videos. They were not charting, just rotating videos. The idea was to use Soviet styling, showing the main symbols of Soviet culture and progress. There are cosmonauts, first satelites, rivers, animals, the construction of multistorey buildings, decorated tablecloths that our parents used to cover TV-sets with when they were off and many other little old-school Russian details.'

MAKING IT
'The multistorey building construction was made in 3Dmax, and the rest was composed and animated in Adobe After Effects.'

ON AIR
'This packaging is one of the most long-lived on MTV Russia. I am grateful to see it has been on air for more than two years.'

TOTALNOE SHOW

MTV RUSSIA

SERGEY PODZOLKOV

ATTITUDE: 'This is what I do perfectly. I want people to change their aims in life, to make them see the world in a different way.'
LOCATION: Moscow, Russia
CLIENTS: MTV, Reebok, Fosters, Gillette, Sony, Panasonic.

MTV CREATIVE DIRECTOR: Ilya Bachurin
DIRECTOR: Sergey Podzolkov

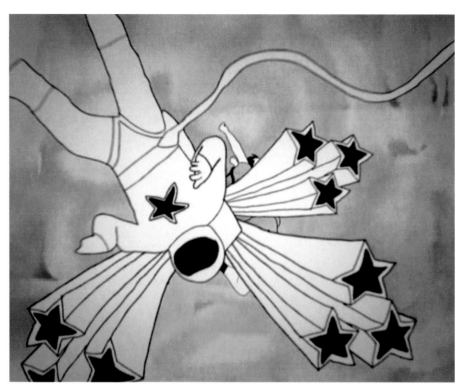

CONCEPT

'The promo of Total Show was created to make people feel alive and happy. The watercolours for these backgrounds were given to me by my five-year old son. The inspiration for the clip was my own. The commission came first but there was no brief involved.'

MAKING IT

'It took me less than a week to make this piece. The most time-consuming part was making the original creative illustrations. The preparation took 70 per cent of the time. I then used Adobe Photoshop and Adobe After Effects to put it all together.'

ON AIR

'The most interesting creative work I do is being aired on MTV. Total Show was the main interactive show on MTV Russia in 2004.'

CENTRE OF RUSSIAN ROCK TITLE SEQUENCE

MTV RUSSIA

SERGIY MELNYK

ATTITUDE: 'To explore the world which lies beyond reality.'
LOCATION: Dubai, United Arab Emirates
CLIENTS: MTV Networks, Motorola, Nike, Panasonic, Samsung, Gillette, MBC, JVC, O'Neill, Kyivstar GSM

CONCEPT, DIRECTION, ANIMATION: Sergiy Melnyk
MUSIC: Aria

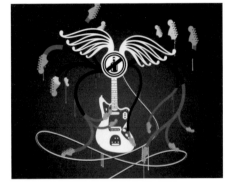

CONCEPT

'I made this when I was working at MTV Russia. Before coming up with a concept I asked a friend of mine – a former rocker and punk – for advice. He told me about the symbols of Russian rock. Usually at rock concerts there are symbols; a circle with a line through it over a bull, a gun or a bottle of alcohol. These signs represent an attitude of peace without crime, without alcohol and without violence. I took the signs as key elements and tried to visualise the title sequence in an up-to-date graphic style.'

MAKING IT

'It took me about a week to finish everything. I used Adobe Illustrator to create all the shapes and Adobe After Effects to animate them. By the end I had discovered other methods to animate vector shapes.'

ON AIR

'I learned a lot whilst working at MTV. I had so much freedom and experimented all the time and now I'm not so constrained in my thoughts.'

MTV VIDEO MUSIC AWARDS 2002, BEST DIRECTION IN A VIDEO

MTV US

JEN RODDIE

ATTITUDE: 'Problem solving through concepts; we're not very good decorators.'
LOCATION: New York, USA
CLIENTS: MTV Networks, Spike TV, Stop Smiling magazine, Guggenheim Museum, RCA Records, Sobe Records, Dreamworks Records

MTV SVP ON AIR DESIGN AND OFF AIR: Jeffrey Keyton
MTV SVP ON AIR PROMOS: Kevin Mackall
DIRECTOR, ART DIRECTOR: Jen Roddie
GRAPHIC DESIGNERS: Clint Woodside, Luke H. Choi
PRODUCER: Jen Roddie
MOONMAN PRODUCTS: Kevin O'Callaghan, Mark Cadicamo, The School of Visual Arts, New York
AFTER EFFECTS ANIMATION: Luke H. Choi, Beth Reinisch
DOP, PACKAGING EDITOR: Todd Antonio Somodevilla
WRITER: Laura Murphy
SOUND DESIGN: Ohm Lab
DESIGN DIRECTOR: Romy Mann
VP DESIGN: Jeffrey Keyton

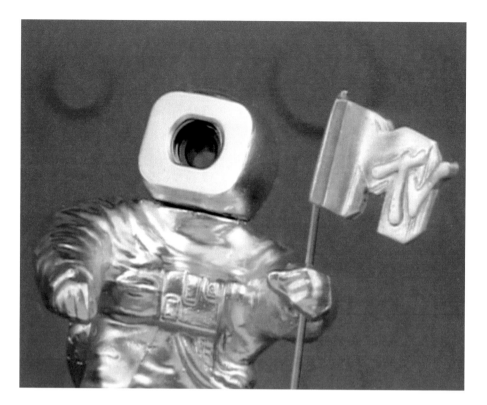

CONCEPT

'To introduce the nominees for the 2002 Video Music Awards, we decided it would be extremely irreverent to make fun of our own award statue and come up with other "functional" uses besides collecting dust on a winners' shelf. Actual award size "moon men" were transformed into functioning appliances and infomercial products that conceptually suited each category; a sprinkler (best dance), rock'em sock'em robots (best rock), sausage maker (best male), and nutcracker (best female) were just a few. We then shot 15" mini-infomercial style pieces showing each product and all of its amazing uses! Some were accompanied by voice-overs or a jingle, while others were simply underscored by music.'

MAKING IT

'The length of this project was about three months from start to finish. There were many challenges; all of the ideas and written copy for each moon man product had to be approved by numerous people before we could start making them. Once approved, we worked with product designers Kevin O'Callaghan and Mark Cadicamo (along with 3D design students) to figure out how functional they could be when shooting, since we wanted to include actual narrative actions, some involving food. The moon men took approximately four weeks to build, all 17 and we shot for two days in a studio.'

ON AIR

'It received great feedback and won awards. But the biggest impact is that it became a huge 3D product design project for the students at the School of Visual Arts in NYC. After making the 17 moon men Kevin O'Callaghan expanded on it and, with his students, created an exhibition of over 200 moon men products. Their exhibition has travelled all over the world.'

POPPED
TITLE SEQUENCE

MTV UK

DARREN GROUCUTT / BERMUDA
SHORTS

ATTITUDE: 'To get the best out of each job; stretching ideas and concepts.'
LOCATION: London, UK
CLIENTS: Wrigleys, Mercedes, Channel 4, Volkswagen, Discovery Channel, Liberty of London, BBC, Classical Brit Awards 2004, Saatchi & Saatchi

MTV HEAD OF CREATIVE: Georgia Cooke
DIRECTOR, ANIMATION: Darren Groucutt
CHARACTER ANIMATION:
Roland Edwards
PRODUCER: Lisa Hill
MUSIC: Adelphoi

CONCEPT

'The clip is the title sequence for a programme called "Popped". A 2D girl walks down the street in a ghetto. A guy in a car drives by and then she passes a group of kids. One kid, showing off, blows some bubble gum and his head floats up, the bubble gum pops and his head falls to the floor and his mates laugh. As the girl gets to the end of the street we see the word Popped written on the wall. The brief was to design a title sequence that had simplicity and that resembled old-style computer graphics. From the initial designs there were only a few alterations before we created something that MTV were happy with.'

MAKING IT

'The main challenge was the character design; creating figures using such a simple design style that had attitude. We employed a character animator to work on them. It took a month to make using Macs. From it we learned how strong a simple visual style could be'.

ON AIR

'Since the clip was aired on MTV, we have had requests for similar work. MTV still has a reputation for being a cool client to work for and creating a title sequence for an up-to-date music programme has given us the opportunity to add something fresh to our showreel. They are different from other clients in that they are creatively aware and fun to work with and you feel like you're working as a team.'

TITLE

MAKE A DIFFERENCE
TUNE-IN

REGION

MTV ASIA PACIFIC

ARTIST

MARK HILLMAN/EARTHTREE
(PTE LTD)

ATTITUDE: 'Actually we are not creative, we just never give up. Our goal is to get paid for fooling about. At heart we are interventionists.'
LOCATION: Singapore
CLIENTS: MTV Asia, Nickelodeon, Golden Village Cinemas, Mediacorp

CREDITS

MTV DIRECTOR, ON AIR PROMOTIONS, CREATIVE AND CONTENT: Charmaine Choo
EXECUTIVE PRODUCER, DIRECTOR, WRITER, SOUND DESIGN: Mark Hillman
ANIMATION DIRECTOR: Sheena Aw
ANIMATOR: Veron Lim
ON-LINE EDITORS: Hentie Heng, Sai Zom Pha

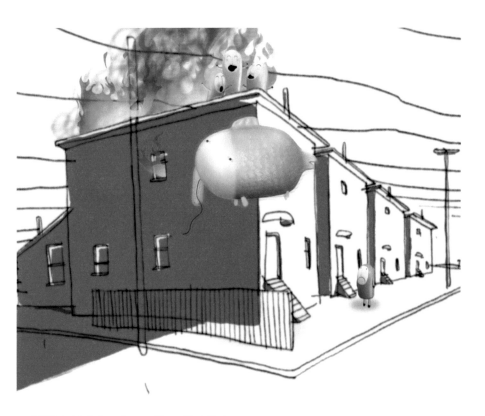

CONCEPT

'The piece was commissioned by Charmaine Choo at MTV who wanted to get viewers to tune in for a new show called "Make a Difference". This show was designed to encourage Singaporean kids to speak their minds on important issues that mattered to them. I wrote a script, did the sound design and had Rob Middleton do the voice over. Then some nice Danish chaps, who we sadly never got to meet or speak to, designed the 3D characters. There seemed to be great potential for these characters to encounter terrible misfortunes. The gag is that whatever they do they just seem to make things worse for each other, with the exception of the hero who at the end brings another character back from the dead just before his ambulance goes over a precipice.'

MAKING IT

'The main challenge was time. We had to complete the animation in three days including revisions and changes. We used After Effects which was not ideal for doing this kind of 2D character animation. I couldn't have pulled it off without Sheena and Veron who completed the job in the middle of composing and animating a twenty-episode show called "Cows and Crayons" that was itself already way behind schedule.'

ON AIR

'Everyone we show the clip to laughs and thinks it's cute. I'd say this was one of the jobs that helped to turn us from an Asian sweatshop into a company you could happily come to for any kind of creative work involving the moving image. I hope I'm not tempting fate here but our relationship with MTV seems to get stronger and stronger. When people talk about clients it sounds distant, as though one could hide behind a brand name. The reality is that you deal with individuals and on this project we were dealing with Charmaine Choo. She's one tough cookie and never gives up trying to improve the work, an attitude I have a lot of time for. We're obviously really keen to have MTV as a client but wonder if we would have done the job as well for a different commissioner.'

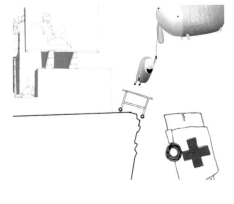

THE BUSINESS OF BEING CREATIVE

CRISTIÁN JOFRÉ
INTERVIEW: MATT HANSON

MTV's greatest transformation has been from a television channel that plays music videos, to being one that becomes a soundtrack for your life. As Creative Director of MTV International, Cristián Jofré is creating the playlist.

'I don't want ideas coming from a computer. The computer gives solutions, not concepts. I don't want to see concept boards and presentations. I think too much broadcasting comes from the screen. Not enough creatives are taking the screen out and thinking about paper and writing and something we can discuss. They are thinking about plug-ins and books that you buy.'

'I am pushing for new ideas. I have a journalistic way of approaching this. Sometimes the designer approaches this from a very convoluted level, talking about the colours, the way they are going to do the promo. But what I want to know is; what is the final idea?'

Cristián Jofré's remit is to push MTV's creativity as far as possible. A Chilean native, with a background in journalism and advertising, Jofré first brought his copywriting skills to MTV Latin America based in Miami. He then helped launch further channels for the MTV stablemate, Nickelodeon, before returning to MTV in 2003 and moving to London and MTV International (MTVi). His main task within the International department is to invigorate the creative environments within the whole of MTV's global family of channels.

He does this through constant communication with Channel Creative Directors, by facilitating the exchange of creative ideas through a company-wide extranet and by organising conferences so that these directors meet each other. And although he might not be a fan of the software plug-ins that enable anyone to create standard visual effects – the anathema to his creative approach – Jofré's department acts as an elite creative squad making 'content plug-ins' to mix up and mutate programming for local channels.

Within MTV's decentralised structure of localised channels, Jofré's roving role is focused on sharing programming ideas and enabling inspiration throughout the network. MTV's parent company Viacom recently soared past the 100-channel mark, with MTV contributing almost half of this total through its regional and localised output. That's a huge amount of programming to keep relevant. Jofré keeps on top of it from within a London office suffused with online connectivity, random gadgetry and broadcast monitors playing the cream of the 10,000 spots produced by MTV's network each year.

'We need to have point of view', states Jofré. *'Because you will never have an audience asking why you don't do more social stuff. We want to have more social content; we believe it is the right thing to do. I think every channel is responsible locally for their image, this is not something for international concern. We don't have a style police department saying; "I don't like the image in India, those images are bad". The responsibility is upon the local departments'.*

While MTV International focuses on driving ideas, and making sure each station is zeroing in on its own original edge, the Creative Directors for every channel are free to select content in co-ordination with their heads of channel and marketing. The mantra is one of 'they decide and we deliver'.

MTVi produces packages that can play through all nations and regions. Sometimes these are purely visual ideas, such as the massive Art Break programme, or they are social and political campaigns on a wide range of hot-button topics.

This mediation between issues, which resonate at local, national and international levels, is an attribute that allows MTV as a channel to transcend the mostly ephemeral nature of its core programming. Music videos are placed amidst a context of radical and emotive ideas.

Jofré acknowledges this intuitively; *'Local stuff is very important. For example, in India they only put on Indian clips. Visually, they have their own looks. Indonesia, or the Philippines, have their own on-air look that belongs solely to them. Local autonomy is very important for keeping the channels relevant. We say, "around the globe, but around the corner", we want to have these two things at the same time, be very local but also global; "glocal". There are very few channels or brands that can say they are truly international, but we can. MTV in one country, such as Thailand, looks entirely different from any other MTV, such as the USA.'*

MTV may also offer up different ideas and solutions to stablemates, but within the context of the MTV brand this is a mark of positive diversity.

The array of ideas that complement this visual framework is the essence of MTV's vitality. In this pursuit of the new, of fresh concepts to outshine the stale formats of other stations in a hyper-competitive multi-channel world, MTV utilises everyone, from in-house creatives, external design companies, and students.

Jofré explains; *'People think they can come to MTV and do whatever they want, but we are a channel with deadlines. We have to make compromises when we generate concepts because we have clients involved; it is a business after all. I like freedom, but I don't like anarchy; I think there's a big difference. I push for freedom and, in the end, when I hire people to work in a specific part of this company, I've already checked out their style. I want them to produce what they are good at.'*

Jofré's role is a balancing act and a tricky one; how to market rebellion, while keeping control of this value; how to utilise it to engage an international, predominantly youthful audience. He sees creative liberty as one of the primary factors in bringing in contributors to this massive effort so as to generate free-flowing ideas. *'We choose the right people and maximise what they do. They feel good because we trust them, they're not going to make as much money sometimes, but we are going to have fun in the end. We have a creative relationship with the people. I don't care in the end about storyboards and all these processes that other clients might be obsessed with. I care about the creativity. In terms of the approval process, we are a lot more flexible than other companies; and at the same time, the potential scope for this creative*

work is valuable, too, not many companies can offer global exposure. I know that this excites people who want to do work for us; they want people to see their work; that is a big difference that not many channels can offer.'

MTV has always traded on its strong voice, and it is this sense of attitude and individualism that creatives must bring to the show. *'I hate to commission stuff. I don't want companies to pitch me ideas. I want to tell them a bit about what I'm going for.'* If the style of the company is right for a project, and Jofré is aware of them, he prefers to initiate contact and collaboration directly. In this way, he is getting the best out of the company and they aren't artificially altering their style in order to get a commission. *'I never go to a meeting blankly. I don't like to see companies on a blind pitch, without a definite reason for seeing them. I always want to have at least some internal process first, a pretext to meet the company. Then I'll go and chose the right company to execute it.'*

'A lot of people send me stuff ready-made for MTV. I don't accept those things, because I want to be part of the creative process. I want them to send me something more personal, and then develop that idea together to create something new. I want to interact with them and have a creative relationship.'

So how does Jofré find inspiration to achieve this state of equilibrium between the creative parameters of MTV and its commercial imperatives?

'I have to shuffle inspiration. Sometimes it's the Internet, sometimes movies, conversations or walks. I don't do brainstorming; it's too structured. Sometimes you don't feel like it, it's not about having one hour to be creative. Personally, in ten years of brainstorming I've never had a good idea. In general, I think people get good ideas when they are on a bus, watching television, or even in a dream. As a creative director, I don't feel the pressure of having ideas. The young guys who work here, they have the ideas.'

By filtering these ideas, he blesses the ones that will fly within MTV's post-modern screenscape, where non-linearity reigns, where opposites attract, a world of anti-commissioning and non-nar-

rative. In many ways, MTV is the antithesis of what commercial broadcasting should be about.

'Perhaps we make nonsense, but we know we are making nonsense. I always need a pretext. I need something that is summarised; give me a title, I need the title. I think journalistically. I take a title and then see the first three lines, then I start writing. I don't want to get the script out. I want to know the idea. I think one of the big challenges we have right now is putting ideas into graphics. The aesthetic point of view isn't enough. I don't want to do beautiful stuff, anyone can do that.'

In a digital world where anyone with the software, manual and inclination can produce top-end animation, ideas have become a premium for Jofré. *'There's all these plug-ins available, everyone's doing motion graphics. I think it's a big challenge right now, to have more than beauty in graphics, to communicate more directly with people. It's not about 20 seconds of beauty.'*

So, how does MTV move forward in a visually saturated culture where ideas are chewed up and spat out at an ever-increasing pace?

'With uncertainty; the day I can define what MTV is going to do, is the day I should quit. I came to MTV when it was playing David Bowie, Radiohead, and all that. Now from Marilyn Manson to 50 Cent, MTV is always changing. We are changing as the audience and music changes; it's at the heart of everything we do.'

The MTV Generation has now moved beyond the boundaries of the television screen. As the MTV network reaches around the globe, conquering the external world, Jofré perceives that the next major challenge for the channel is in conquering those virtual worlds currently blossoming around us.

'My competitor is the Internet. People are now spending more time on the Internet than watching television. The big change happening now is that we are going from viewers to users. Users can download, upload, shape, customise, interact; it's not a static thing anymore. Our next step is to move towards these new platforms and devices.'

TITLE

RUSSIA TOP 10

REGION

MTV RUSSIA

ARTIST

ANTON SAKARA

ATTITUDE: 'For me it is vital to create
things that find a consumer.'
LOCATION: Moscow, Russia
CLIENTS: 1st State Channel of Russia,
Channel Russia, MTV Russia, MTV Central
Europe, Fox Italy, McCann Ericsson, Darcy

CREDITS

MTV CREATIVE DIRECTOR: Ilya Bachurin
DESIGN, ANIMATION, SOUND:
Anton Sakara

CONCEPT

'The brief came at really short notice, I had about
one week to do the work. The show presents the
best of Russian video clips, so I chose the theme of
the game Tetris, which was originally created by
Russian computer programmers. I see Russian pop
music as something that is growing but has not yet
achieved its final shape. That's why there is a feeling of art-digital chaos while the blocks of Tetris
are being assembled.

ON AIR

'The piece evoked different reactions. MTV creatives were crazy about it, but some colleagues from
other Russian tv-channels said it was too provocative and its graphics did not correspond to the
show's content. The music videos that are rotating
inside this packaging are not as progressive and
bold in style. Perhaps such a reaction is a good sign,
suggesting that I was on the right path!'

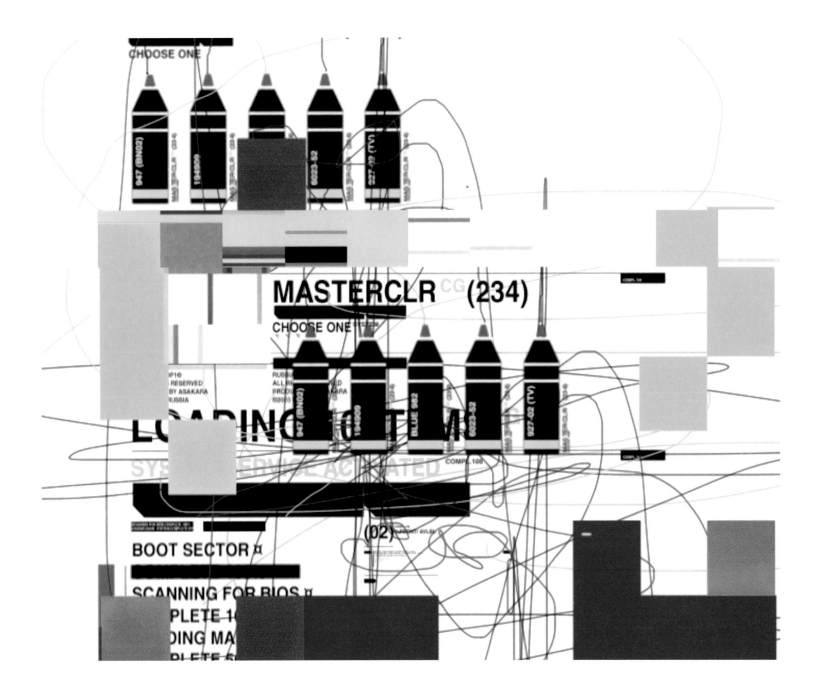

TITLE

consensus
tune-in

REGION

MTV Japan

ARTIST

Tak (Taku) Inoue

LOCATION: Japan
CLIENTS: MTV, Boom Satellites, Crimson
Labyrinth Dragon Ash, OAP, Presto

CREDITS

MTV EXECUTIVE PRODUCER ON AIR
PROMOS AND CREATIVE: Miyako Hattori
DIRECTOR: Tak (Taku) Inoue
MUSIC: Tetsu Kubota

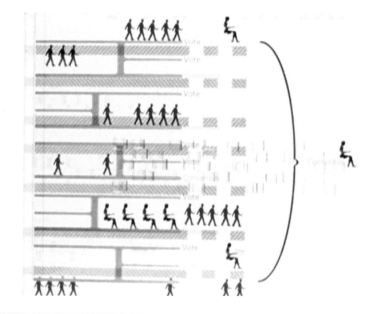

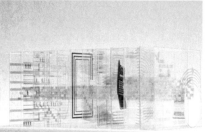

CONCEPT

'The key part of making this clip was the sensational feeling of it being handcrafted. When we were figuring out how to make the word "Concensus" look like 3D letters, the entire staff concentrated on working it out together. Indeed, this was a great moment of real concensus!'

MAKING IT

'During shooting, the tiny acrylic cubes that the letters were made of fell apart in the heat of the lights, so the model needed to be reassembled at the shoot. We used 16mm film and Turntable. This is one of the few really satisfying clips I have made because the end-result expressed a much prettier world than I had imagined.'

ON AIR

'The clip was commissioned by MTV Japan and it is edited just for that region. We haven't heard anything directly, but apparently the clip was well-received overseas. Actually, I don't usually have enough time to think about past projects because I'm always too busy with the next one.'

TITLE

RUSSIA TOP 20
PROMO

REGION

MTV RUSSIA

ARTIST

SERGIY MELNYK

ATTITUDE: 'To explore the world which lies beyond reality.'
LOCATION: Dubai, United Arab Emirates
CLIENTS: MTV Networks, Motorola, Nike, Panasonic, Samsung, Gillette, MBC, JVC, O'Neill, Kyivstar GSM

CREDITS

MTV CREATIVE DIRECTOR: Ilya Bachurin
CONCEPT, DIRECTION, ANIMATION: Sergiy Melnyk
MUSIC: My Robot Friend

CONCEPT

'I was given the task of creating a promo based on photos of doves by Sergey Podzolkov. The doves had to be numbered, representing the Top 20 music artists (from an idea by Andrei Bumagin). I came up with an idea of exploding the doves into bricks. I had to fit the promo to the style of a title sequence for the Top 20 show that was made by Sergey Zavyalov, so I made vectorized bricks.'

MAKING IT

'It took me between four and five days to create this promo. I used Discreet 3Dmax to make the 3D bricks, Adobe Illustrator to create the vector elements and Adobe After Effects to compose the graphics with the photos.'

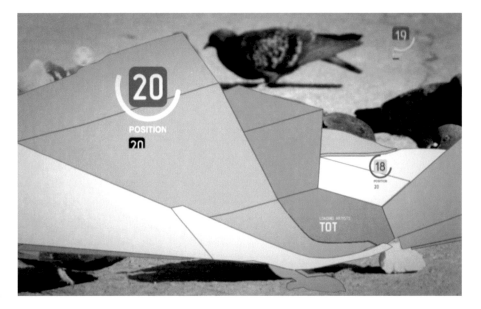

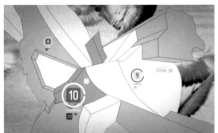

TITLE

FAVOURITE VIDEOS SHOW

REGION

MTV RUSSIA

ARTIST

ANTON SAKARA

ATTITUDE: 'For me it is vital to create things that find a consumer.'
LOCATION: Moscow, Russia
CLIENTS: 1st State Channel of Russia, Channel Russia, MTV Russia, MTV Central Europe, Fox Italy, McCann Ericsson, Darcy

CREDITS

MTV CREATIVE DIRECTOR: Ilya Bachurin
3D DESIGN, ANIMATION: Anton Sakara
SOUND: Oleg Litvishko

CONCEPT

'This clip was made for a show about the favourite videos of an invited celebrity. The idea was based on contact between a big robot and little spheres. The big robot saves the little spheres and gives them life by putting its shaft inside of them. The little spheres start feeling love after big robot has touched them. This represents the idea of the show: MTV and a presenter make a guest celebrity reveal what videos they really love by probing them with questions.'

MAKING IT

'The 3D forms and shapes were inspired by the observation of car tail-lights in long, night-time traffic-jams in Moscow. The spot was made using 3Dmax, VRay and Adobe After Effects.'

ON AIR

'The impact of this piece was revealed when a bunch of replicas were made less than a year after this packaging was released, some of them on MTV and some not.'

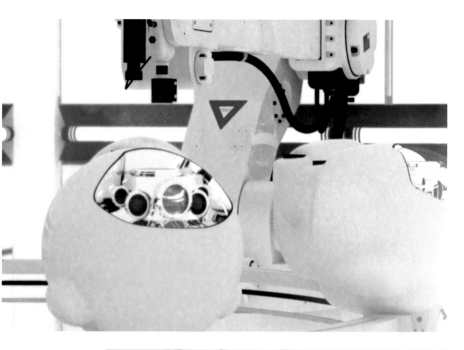

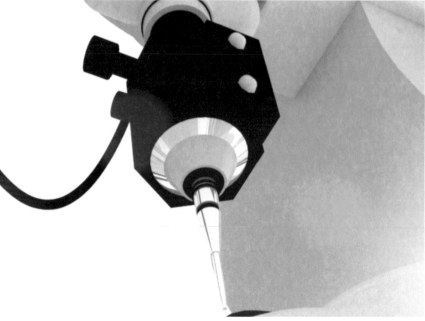

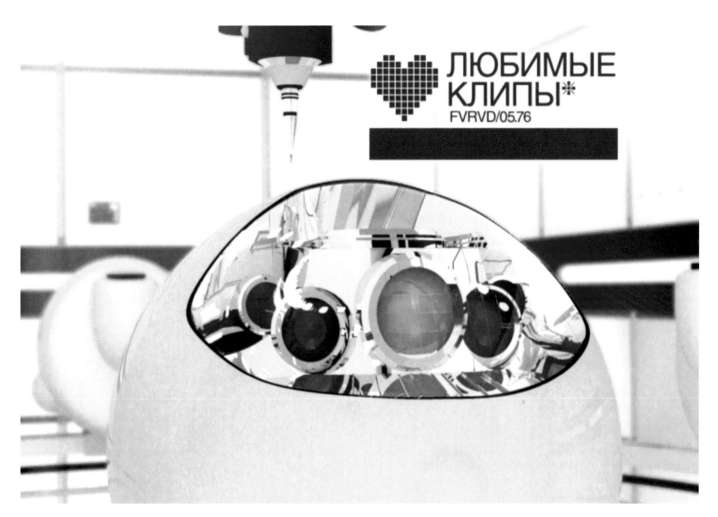

ЛЮБИМЫЕ
КЛИПЫ*
FVRVD/05.76

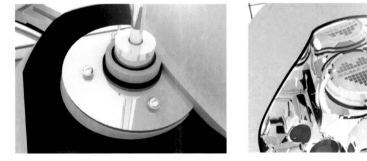

TITLE

BRAND NEW

REGION

MTV ASIA

ARTIST

TATIANA AROCHA

ATTITUDE: 'To come up with work that leaves people happy and inspired.'
LOCATION: New York, USA
CLIENTS: VH1, CMT, MTV, Expansion Team, Wieden & Kennedy, Nike

CREDITS

MTV DIRECTOR, ON AIR PROMOTIONS, CREATIVE AND CONTENT: Charmaine Choo
DIRECTOR: Tatiana Arocha
3D: Carlos Ivan Molina
PRODUCTION COMPANY:
The Ebeling Group
EXECUTIVE PRODUCER: Mick Ebeling
PRODUCER: Sue Lee

CONCEPT

'This piece was inspired by urban environments. There was a brief and an existing piece to refer to. MTV wanted a version that had the same feeling but was new and cool. The piece needed to be abstract and simple but have dynamic motion and feel like it was evolving. I was commissioned by the Ebeling Group to design and creatively direct the project and they were hired by MTV. The work is a whole show package, this clip is the opening sequence for the package.'

MAKING IT

'The main challenge was to find a balance between an abstract concept and some type of narrative. The schedule was very short, it took around three weeks to make. I worked on a G4 dual processor and I hired my friend Carlos Ivan Molina to help me with the 3D. He is very good with Maya and we had worked in Colombia together, so it was a good project to bring him onto.'

ON AIR

'I treat MTV the same as all my clients, I take each job separately and I work with the client very closely to get the best results for their product.'

SCHLINGENSIEF'S U3000

MTV CENTRAL

TIM BLISS / FROGSTAR, STEPHAN SCHOMERUS

ATTITUDE: 'To find what is not obvious and to avoid visual noise. My mission is to avoid clichés and to put light into darkness, just like the moon.' (T. Bliss)
LOCATION: Berlin, Germany
CLIENTS: MTV, RESfest, Cinefeel

CREDITS

MTV HEAD OF ON AIR: Thomas Sabel
DIRECTOR: Stephan Schomerus
DESIGN, ANIMATION: Tim Bliss
MUSIC: Frogstar

CONCEPT

T. Bliss: 'The idea came from Stephan Schomerus who was a colleague of mine. I basically rendered multiple scenes in different formats and later Stephan put it together.'

MAKING IT

T. Bliss: 'The funny thing about the piece is that I built a subway train in 3D, with loads of detail on the inside. Most of my time was spent trying to make the interior photo-realistic. But we only ended up using exterior shots and different mapping, so all the effort to detail the train on the inside was wasted. I guess I learned that no matter what you think you are making, it will mutate of its own accord, which is good because if you hate what you're working on in the beginning, you will probably end up liking what you did to correct it. MTV is often a place where you can make things happen and it is good for that.'

ON AIR

T. Bliss: 'The first job I did for MTV was in 1996 for MTV Latin America and it won a silver award. This made a huge impact on my reel at the time and helped me realise that MTV is great for having fun while you work, but not always of course.'

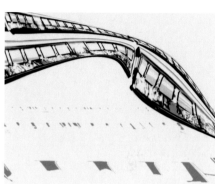

COORDINATES BEAUTY

MTV INTERNATIONAL

FERNANDO LAZZARI, MELISSSA SILVERMAN, OLEG TROYANOVSKY

ATTITUDE: 'Solving communication problems within a given framework.'
(F. Lazarri)
LOCATION: Miami, USA
CLIENTS: MTV Latin America, MTV All International regions, Vh1 Latin America, VH1 US, Canal 13 Argentina, TyC Sports Argentina, other channels in Argentina

MTV CREATIVE DIRECTOR: Cristian Jofre
DIRECTORS: Melissa Silverman,
Oleg Troyanovsky, Fernando Lazzari
GRAPHICS PRODUCER: Patty Arana
PHOTOGRAPHY: Many photographers around the world
MUSIC: Nortec Collective

CONCEPT

F. Lazarri: 'Melissa Silverman from MTV US came up with this idea at the end of 2001. We wanted to illustrate the meaning of different words around the world, and their interpretation in different cultures by various artists. Photographers from all over the world were given a word from an international list. They would submit photos based on that word (for example, Beauty or Silence or Sex) which then would be sent to an MTV region (eg. Russia) and their producers would put together a spot using all the pictures for that word. We wanted to communicate where each picture came from, but writing the names of the cities seemed too distracting and obvious. So we came up with the idea of using coordinates. Instead of saying, "this picture is from Brazil" we said, "this picture is from some remote place in the world", and in this way it would give scope for more imagination. Also, I think it gave a very poetic feeling to the campaign. For the typography, we had to translate each word into twenty different languages and lay the type in such a way that you can see them all mix with the global concept. This was a great challenge, because not only were we dealing with words of completely different lengths, but were also mixing typography (Roman, Chinese, Arabic, Indian) within the same layout. For each spot we used one main colour and a different piece of music.'

MAKING IT

F. Lazarri: 'Once the strategy for the campaign was decided, making each piece was not particularly challenging. I put together all the images in After Effects, and the challenge was in the editing, picking up the right order for the pictures and figuring out when to go back to graphics, the framing of the pictures and the cut speed in relation to the music.

ON AIR

F. Lazarri: 'Everyone liked this campaign. I think it's because of the poetic feeling. This was a sort of an independent idea from inside the company, and of course we had all the freedom in the world to produce it.'

51°N, 0°W

bellezza
45°N, 9°E

47°N, 19°E

21°N, 79°W

19°N, 72°E

ความงาม
14°N, 126°E

34°S, 58°W

23°S, 46°W

CAMPUS INVASION TITLE SEQUENCE

MTV CENTRAL

BENJAMIN BRETTSCHNEIDER

ATTITUDE: 'Being creative is one of the most pleasurable ways to make some bucks; and apart from that I wouldn't know how to do anything else.'
LOCATION: Berlin, Germany
CLIENTS: MTV, Pro7, RTL, Independent Film Festival UK

MTV HEAD OF ON AIR: Thomas Sabel
IDEA, DIRECTION, EDITING AND GFX: Benjamin Brettschneider
PRODUCTION COMPANY: BSW Film
DOP: Claus Bosch Dos Santos
PRODUCTION MANAGER: Jens Bruhn
PRODUCER: Markus Wacker
FIRST AD: Philip Haferbusch
SOUND: Jim Griffin / Soho Studios (title sequence), Chris Turner (promos)

CONCEPT

'Campus Invasion is a big open-air live event that takes place at universities, so my idea was to show the opposite, empty, dark places in a university and the silence before the storm. Since MTV does not usually give you an exact brief, you start to develop ideas from scratch, which is fun because it gives you a lot of creative freedom. This title sequence is part of a whole package (closer, bumpers, etc.) and a promo campaign, which included an actor next to the typography. Over the years I have made over a dozen different trailers from the material.'

MAKING IT

'It took a long time to find the right location and eventually we found it at Hamburg University, where we were allowed to film for two days. The building had the perfect cool atmosphere of typical German post-War architecture. Alongside the superb camera man Claus Bosch Dos Santos, and the fantastic team at BSW Film in Hamburg, the then production manager of MTV Central, Jens Bruhn, helped me throughout the project and made it possible to do a shoot like this with little money. And off course there was Peter Moller, the creative director of MTV Central until 2003. He was the one who gave me the job and inspired me. I did the post-production in After Effects. Since I had no tracking points I had to do it all by eye, trying to match the perspective and movements manually. It took some time but after a few days I became quite comfortable with putting text on a wall and having it moving.'

ON AIR

'The feedback was very satisfying. The packaging and the promos, which were generated from the same material, were used for three seasons. At the time that it went on air, the German TV Station Pro7 was working on a new on-air design that also involved floating type in 3D space. They called me and asked for some samples to watch during their compositing. Just recently I saw an image film for a mobile phone company that used the same style and similar shots; so I guess some people liked the work.'

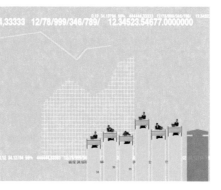

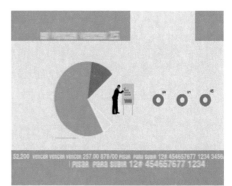

TITLE

VIDEO MUSIC BRAZIL 2002
OPENING SEQUENCE

REGION

MTV BRAZIL

ARTIST

AMIR ADMONI,
PAULA ORDONHES

ATTITUDE: 'To tease people, and hopefully make them laugh too, about our lives and the world we live in.'
LOCATION: São Paulo, Brazil
CLIENTS: MTV Brazil

CREDITS

MTV PROMO MANAGER: Rodrigo Pimenta
DIRECTORS, PRODUCERS:
Amir Admoni, Paula Ordonhes
EXECUTIVE PRODUCER: Jimmy Leroy
ACTOR, COLLABORATOR: Leandro Lima
MUSIC: Adriano Cintra

CONCEPT

'This piece is part of a graphic package produced by the promo department of MTV Brazil for Video Music Brazil 2002, which is the main event produced by MTV in this country. The main concept was to show (and satirize) the event by presenting it as a corporation and the artists as its clients. We designed logos for each band, singer, presenter and host of the show. They were shown in fake outdoor environments digitally placed in urban landscapes to generate the pieces that introduced each competition category. The idea of the opening sequence was to make fun of the stereotypical corporation and its mannerisms such as competition, hierarchy, standardisation, hard-to-achieve goals, coffee breaks and phoney smiles.'

MAKING IT

'The main challenge was to make it with no money, that's why we shot Leandro Lima, our actor and promo colleague, on Chroma Key and later multiplied and placed him in a graphic environment made with After Effects. It was quite simple to make, in fact the hardest part was coming up with the idea.'

ON AIR

'MTV Brazil has an inhouse promo department of about 15 designers and producers working full-time on broadcast pieces. I am part of the team so I don't really have other clients that I work for. Usually there are no restrictions concerning the content of the pieces, only if the end result looks too embarrassing. That was not the case with this one, though.'

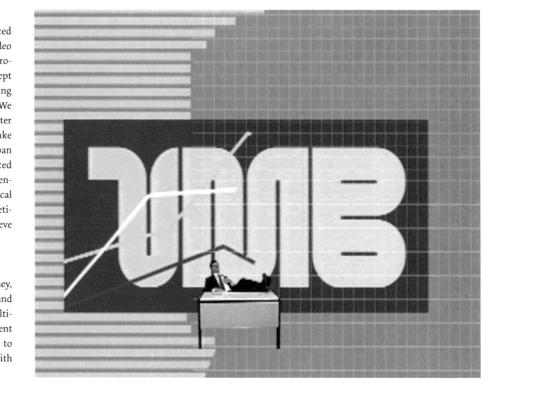

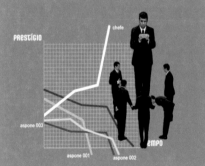

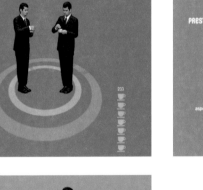

ROCKER

MTV CENTRAL

CRAIG ROBINSON

ATTITUDE: 'Pretty music, pictures, people and dogs...and the desire to do something better than the last thing I did.'
LOCATION: Berlin, Germany
CLIENTS: Observer Music Magazine, MTV, Esquire, XFM, Time Out, Radiotimes.com, FNAC

CREDITS

MTV HEAD OF ON AIR: Thomas Sabel
DIRECTOR: Craig Robinson
MUSIC: The Haunted

CONCEPT

'I was working at a company called Defcom and we were building the website for MTV Germany. One of my colleagues had done a quick scribble of a pixel character. I began to play with it and suggested it be used on the website to inject a tiny detail, a bit of humour. The client liked it and asked us to make television clips to advertise the website. In total there were eight clips, each of which focused on a different genre of music. I also made a four-part series for Valentine's Day.'

MAKING IT

'The main challenges were that I had no experience in making anything other than animated GIFs at that point, so I put it all together in Director to work out the timing, then used a video editing program to put each picture together. It was quite a tedious process.'

ON AIR

'People seemed to like it. The client liked the Nanopops, and I've done work for MTV since then, so I must have done something right. We did some versions for MTV in Spain too.'

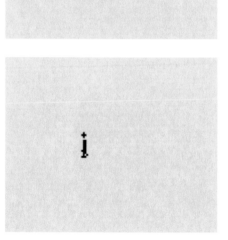

BLOQUE INTERACTIVO IDS

MTV LATIN AMERICA

DOMA

ATTITUDE: 'Playing like kids. Something we love to do is to create New Universes and play God.'
LOCATION: Buenos Aires, Argentina
CLIENTS: MTV, Locomotion Channel, Sony AXN, Discovery, Animal Planet, Disney Channel

CREDITS

MTV DIRECTOR, ON AIR:
Alejandro Abramovich
ART DIRECTOR, SCRIPT:
Julian Pablo Manzelli / Doma
ANIMATORS: J.P. Manzelli, John Lum
SOUND DESIGN: Mariano Dabini

CONCEPT

'Alejandro Abramovich and Pepe Carmona, from MTV Latin America, put together a group of artists (Julian Pablo Manzelli, Matias Vigliano, John Lum, Mariano Dabini) to create the Bloque Interactivo packaging. This programme block consists of different interactive TV shows where people can participate via their mobile phones: voting, sending messages and images. We did a number of different pieces for the entire block; interstitials, IDs, menus, bugs. For one of them we were asked to create a series of ID-campaigns to promote the website and call people to participate online. Julian came up with the idea of playing with absurd situations, mixing the click/mouse action/concept with human and crazy gadgets actions, little jokes with the cause and effect structure. The art direction was totally inspired by the pixel illustrations of mobile phones.'

MAKING IT

'To work with pixels is not as easy as it looks. Julian created all the illustrations in Photoshop, tracing photographs and drawing new elements, working pixel by pixel and avoiding blurs. With the help of John Lum, he then animated the series of six IDs. At the end Mariano Dabini designed the audio.'

ON AIR

'We have never received direct feedback from the channel. But there was feedback from friends and people who have watched the clips on air. People really liked them.'

REGION

MTV INDIA

ARTIST

UNTITLED MEDIA PVT LTD

ATTITUDE: 'To stand on this threshold every day can be both excruciatingly painful and ultimately euphoric. These challenges are what drive us creatively and inspire us to continue designing.'
LOCATION: Mumbai, India
CLIENTS: NECC, LML, MTV, Pepsodent, Channel [V], Airtel

CREDITS

MTV VP CREATIVE AND CONTENT:
Cyrus Oshidar
PRODUCER: Sharan Masand
DIRECTOR, DESIGNER: Sarah Hunt
MUSIC: Evanescence

CONCEPT

'This promo was the introduction to the show. It introduced the style that the project would follow and had to contain a lot of information without becoming overly cluttered and confusing. The script was strong but direct, backed up by block text to reinforce the message. We used iconic imagery to set the tone and picked a strong music track to give magnitude to the images shown. MTV outlined the show's formula to us and suggested various approaches. The nature of the show meant that it had to hit the screens with a presence and magnitude that represented the prestige MTV was attaching to the award. After exploring various styles, we decided on the communist propaganda look, as it was very amenable to integrating elements that would give the show a bold visual image. Communist artwork has always depicted the common man in a glorified stance placing all people on an equal footing. This was particularly relevant as the show would involve a mix of high and low profile Indian achievers. This design helped us create a grand, but not elitist, heroic idealisation of all the nominees, irrespective of their fame. The music track set the tone, strong and uplifting but with a darker edge to it. We chose a track from Evanescence, as it and was a recognisable, popular track for the generation that the show was aimed at.'

MAKING IT

'Once we had decided on the style of the project, we researched how to make the communist propaganda look more Indian. We decided to keep a mix of very bold iconic landmarks representing different international architecture to give a global scale. The human elements were shot on Chroma so we could compose them into the frame. All of the models were styled authentically and shot in very typical poses of the genre. We completed the main artwork prior to the shoot so we could place references for angles and magnifications while we were shooting. The project took us about three weeks including the Chroma shoot. We shot on Digi Beta, edited on M-100 and used After Effects to compose and animate. All layout work was done in Photoshop and 3D elements were created using 3D Max.'

ON AIR

'This project has been immensely successful for MTV. The approach was completely different to any other promos on air in India and as a design team we were overwhelmed with the feedback from peers and viewers alike. We were privileged to be a part of this project and are extremely honoured to have won two awards at Promax Asia 2004 for our work. MTV India is one of our favourite clients; they are aware of what they want to communicate and once a format has been decided upon they allow us complete creative freedom.'

YOUR HERÖES

MTV INDONESIA VJ HUNT 2004, CALL FOR ENTRIES

REGION

MTV INDONESIA

ARTIST

RICK SOERAFANI

ATTITUDE: 'MTV, Gue banget!' (MTV, it's so me! MTV Indonesia tagline)
LOCATION: Jakarta, Indonesia
CLIENTS: MTV Indonesia, BNI 46, Amway Indones, TVC

CREDITS

DIRECTOR: Rick Soerafani
GRAPHIC ARTIST: Nala Wiradidjaja
PRODUCTION ASSISTANT: Diandra Amalia
EXECUTIVE PRODUCER: Lesley Desker
PRODUCTION OFFICER: Juli Rochlanawaty
FIRST AD: Syamsurizal
TALENT: Ferdi, Dewi
CAMERAMAN: Hudi Sukarma
VOICE OVER: Aryo Bimo
EDITOR: Eko, Hari and Gunawan
WARDROBE: Marion
MAKE UP: Ani, Dini
MUSIC: Marilyn Manson

CONCEPT

'The clip is a short promo inviting viewers to participate in the upcoming VJ Hunt competition. We were inspired by the fact that it was about the same time as local presidential elections in Indonesia. Therefore the idea was for a propaganda style using the same colours and dramatic angles, way before the release of "Sky Captain And The World Of Tomorrow".

MAKING IT

'The main challenge was the propaganda concept itself. We had to ask ourselves: Do we dare to do this? The concept and preparations for the shoot took about a week, shooting and editing another week. We used a Digital Betacam, AVID and Adobe After Effects. We encountered one problem during shooting, which was the limited size of the green screen in our studio. As a result we learned that a green screen shoot is not as easy as it looks.'

ON AIR

'MTV is cool. Having an MTV clip in my portfolio means that girls think its cool and clients notice me. The clip was commissioned for MTV Indonesia. In terms of restrictions there are no blatant left-wing symbols allowed on air in this country.'

CLUB GENERATION

MTV ITALY

ROBERTO BAGATTI, VERA BRAGHIROLI

ATTITUDE: 'Creativity is first of all about growing up.' (R. Bagatti)
'Have fun and learn.' (V. Braghiroli)
LOCATION: Milan, Italy
CLIENTS: Sky Cinema, McCann Erickson, MTV

CREDITS

DIRECTION: Vera Braghiroli (Promo), Roberto Bagatti (Show Package)
GRAPHIC DESIGNER: Roberto Bagatti
DOP: Sergio De Feudis
PRODUCTION COMPANY: MADE srl
STYLING: Elena Barosi
POST PRODUCTION: 3Dvision, Milan
EDITING VIDEO: Vera Braghiroli/3Dvision
EDITING AUDIO: Mach 2, Milan
MUSIC: AFX, Plump DJs

CONCEPT

R. Bagatti: 'The idea evolved from working on a series of portraits that could describe the generation we were asked to illustrate. I was inspired by club and dance music aesthetics, from clothes to covers, flyers and styling. We wanted to integrate many different visual references that are often part of club iconography but to keep everything clean and sharp. The music is fast and in your face, almost stealth cuts and animations are more a matter of frames than seconds, edited to the beats. There are references to Japanese manga, graffiti, tags and typography mixed with street stencils and sticker art. The initial brief was to make the piece more pop and mainstream but the project eventually moved towards what could be considered one of the most interesting aspects of club culture, the independent, left-field part of it; more street-oriented and open to many influences.'

V. Braghiroli: 'This is about a selection of young guys, 16 to 30 years old, keen on house music who understand the club as being a place where you are not only allowed to express yourself freely, but are expected to show yourself off visually.'

MAKING IT

R. Bagatti: 'It was hard work casting in just a few days and getting all the kids together; then shooting enough material with limited studio time. Everything was produced, shot, designed and post-produced (audio and video) in a rush in order to meet the tight deadline. Because of the limited budget and time available we couldn't really think about anything besides putting together the best work within the restrictions. If there was a challenge that would have been making a bold, hard-hitting sequence out of a series of simple portraits, without

actions from the kids; something that matched up with the AFX track that could be aggressive and rough-edged but also sharp and tight at same time. That is my idea of clubbing, it's not always a pleasant experience but it's drives you to go back and be part of scene.'

V. Braghiroli: 'As with any other project, the main challenge is to stay focused on your goal but also to be flexible enough to turn the inevitable hitches that happen during the progress of events to your own advantage, usually moving inside strict budget and deadline boundaries. It took one week of pre-production, one day of shooting, one day of editing and two days of post-production. The problems were small unexpected events; from the wrong paint colour used on the background limbo to the non-appearance of one of the cast on the morning of shooting and the emergency calls to find a substitute at the very last moment.'

ON AIR

R. Bagatti: 'There was positive feedback from the channel and the audience. I think the Club Generation nights were fairly popular events, with major line-

ups. A whole range of off-air Club Gen material was produced with the graphics designed for on air; flyers, posters, t-shirts and postcards. I have many MTV clips in my portfolio, I spent six years at MTV. Brands like MTV usually speak for themselves, people always seem to be very open towards MTV projects because they perceive them as innovative or up-to-date. It's not a matter of actually having an MTV clip in your portfolio, it's more a matter of having had the opportunity to work for them.'

V. Braghiroli: 'This was the first promo that I had the chance to shoot on film and since other promos have followed, I would say that it has had a positive impact on my work.'

THIS IS OUR MUSIC

MTV NORDIC

MANS SWANBERG / PISTACHIOS

ATTITUDE: 'Worn ideas give me a sinking feeling. So I avoid them, and voilà it's créatif!'
LOCATION: Stockholm, Sweden
CLIENTS: Sony Music, Harpers Bazaar, Wallpaper, Levi's, Edwin Jeans, Penguin Books, Cheap Monday, Tokion, Et Vous, MTV, Vogue Homme

CREDITS

MTV CREATIVE DIRECTOR: Lars Beckung
CONCEPT, ART DIRECTION,
ILLUSTRATION, ANIMATION: Pistachios
PHOTOGRAPHY: Pistachios, Anna Källsen
MUSIC: Maher Shalal Hash Baz

CONCEPT
'The show is about independent artists and their music, so we wanted to reflect that in the graphics. I figured out that cross-stitching shared the hand-made feel and the obsessiveness of music that is made simply because it has to be. And sewing over the photographs would take an established, prefab world and turn it into something personal.'

MAKING IT
'With digital cameras, you get folders piling up on the computer, heaps of photos that have never had much point, until Anna Källsen at MTV took even more photos in LA. The stitches were made with a 3D particle system, which was complicated. At some point I wondered if it would have been less work to actually just sew it, but no, that would have been worse.'

ON AIR
'We have received a lot of good feedback, and some awards; silver at Promax, gold in New York and gold at the Kolla! awards. MTV is a client that creates loads of graphics and knows a lot about it, whereas other clients may have no idea.'

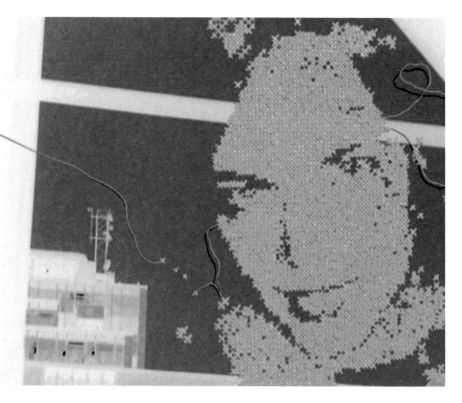

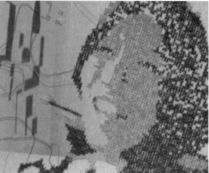

SMF5
(SPORTS AND MUSIC FESTIVAL 5)

MTV US

TODD ST. JOHN / HUNTERGATHERER

LOCATION: New York, USA
CLIENTS: MTV, VH1, Sundance, Nixon, Nike, Surfing, Burton, New York Times, Fuse, 2K

MTV SVP ON AIR DESIGN AND OFF AIR:
Jeffrey Keyton
MTV SVP ON AIR PROMOS: Kevin Mackall
DIRECTOR, DESIGNER: Todd St. John
ADDITIONAL TALENT, VOICES,
CUT-OUT ARTISTS: Gary Benzel,
Robin Hendrickson, Craig Metzger,
Stuart Weiner

CONCEPT
'I had created this same project for MTV for four years running, from SMF2, up to SMF5. It was MTV's version of the X-Games, but with music. Each year the show and budgets got scaled back to the point that I proposed this really low-budget concept. It was based on, or rather stolen from, a video I'd made in high school.'

MAKING IT
'It was made in a day, with in-camera audio. It's pretty much, what you see is what you get.'

ON AIR
'I got a call one day before this was to air, saying the producers had decided not to run it because it was too rough, even though they had seen the process evolve all along. In the end I think that Romy convinced them that it was worth showing, and it ran. After the fact, everybody seemed really into it, which is how it goes some times.'

same
but different

sophie lovell

The bigger MTV gets, the more regions, demographic groups and markets it caters to and the more disparate and divided it becomes, thus the more it needs to concentrate on maintaining an unmistakable core identity. But the big bonus that comes with this exponential growth is the flood of regional creative input, fresh ideas and attitudes. Regional variety is an essential part of the brand's creative development; each region's channels are obviously MTV channels and yet have their own flavours and touches that make them unique; they are individually customised interpretations of MTV.

When MTV launches a new regional channel it tends to follow a sort of speeded up evolution of how the music channel originally started in 1981 beginning with 'link and clip' shows hosted by local VJs and eventually developing into a 'total entertainment' channel. This often means that space for creative and artistic idents gets more and more squeezed the more established the channel becomes and the more valuable the region's airtime becomes.

Maurizio Vitale, former vice president and creative director, MTV South was, until recently, responsible for the MTV channels in Italy, France, Spain and Portugal, each of which is at a different stage in the MTV 'evolution' chain.

'Lets say we have five steps for an MTV channel. The first step is a total music channel; just link and clips and videos. Step five is a total entertainment, youth-oriented people channel, it has got everything: news, shows, live events, concerts, videos and so on. Lets say that Italy is on step five, Portugal is on step one, Spain and France are between step three and step four. Portugal is the one that will benefit the most from idents because it has only one show so far: a link and clip show with a VJ, and the rest is pure programming of American shows, different European shows and loads of music. So in this structure, channel idents play an important role because they identify the channel to the outside world and benefit the image of the channel. Italy on the other hand is a generic entertainment channel, which competes with the other major television channels on an open platform. Right now it has five news shows per day, 18 different show productions, produces around 19 to 25 hours of live shows per week, with 11 VJs plus three guests stars. So within this kind of structure the space available to programme idents is considerably reduced.'

Idents as creative expressions are therefore all the more vital for a channel like MTV Italy, says Vitale, 'An ident is like a little space inside MTV, which is probably the only non-commercial space left on the channel'.

The UK is one of the most crowded, fractured and competitive television markets in the world. Here the channel evolution process has gone a step further. There are five UK MTV channels; the master channel and the genre channels, which focus on music, dance, hits and more. Georgia Cooke, head of UK On-Air at MTV UK says that graphics and idents are essential in establishing and maintaining the clear identities for these channels and distinguishing them from the competition (there are around 28 music channels in the UK) as well as each other.

'MTV, being the mother brand, is much more eclectic and uses a shopping process to look for ideas and to create really unusual and arresting designs intended to break appeal to that particular demographic of 17- to 18-year-old youth. It's much more about brand separation when it comes to the other channels. Although they have the same spirit and attitude at heart, they have to be different from each other so that the audience understands what we are trying to give them. So for us the identity starts to become a really big part of the edge, the difference; that's why we really try and do things first.'

Being 'first', staying ahead of the competition and the imitators is of primary concern to many regions. For some channels this is about being brave enough to step out into the unknown. Georgia Cooke again: 'Personally I think we should always be doing things that scare us while we are making them. The most successful things that we've done in the UK have been the things that have made us stay awake at night thinking, "My God what are we doing?".'

For other markets, the most successful vehicle for bringing MTV closer to the hearts of the viewers is humour. 'Humour travels well', says Lars Beckung, creative director at MTV Nordic. 'We take idents from other countries too and they work well, either on a "yes we have same humour", or on a "oh my God your humour is so funny because it's different" level.'

MTV India has used humour right from the channel's launch in 1996 to define a form of irreverence that works well in their region, and pushes boundaries without shock tactics. Cyrus Oshidar, senior vice president, creative and content, MTV India explains; 'Humour is one of most defining features of MTV India. In Indian culture humour is very slapstick, it's basic stuff and is still very puerile. The attitude at the beginning was not "made in India" but "mad in India". Indians love puns, so we played around with that a lot. It was at the time when the whole liberalisation thing was happening. There was a whole cultural overlay, a change in music, a change in personality, a generational shift was happening. India was changing itself; it was irreverent, funny, and loud and in India you have to be loud to be noticed.'

Humour can build bridges, but it can also divide. Although there is much exchange between regions of hit shows such as 'Pimp my Ride' or 'Dismissed', for certain regions there are forms of Western comedy that are complete no-go areas. Charmaine Choo, director, On-Air promotions, MTV Networks Asia, says that although the main language used in her region is English, that doesn't mean that anything goes in terms of programming from other English-language MTV channels.

'Everything is in English because it's widely used in Malaysia and Singapore. There are Malays, Chinese, Indians and Eurasians living here and most of the international shows like "TRL" and "Punk'd" work well as do the Music Video Awards, but we don't run "Jackass" here, it's too extreme and would require too much censorship. So we have an Asian version of "Jackass" called "MTV Whatever Things" that shows a group of guys doing mad stunts all over Asia.'

Likewise in India, where for all its irreverent humour there are still distinct lines that are not to be crossed, says Cyrus Oshidar; 'We have a candid camera show called "Bakra", which means "scapegoat". That's our version of Jackass, but we don't do crass stuff. If we ran Jackass I'd be in jail.'

Strangely enough, English-language humour is a completely different issue for MTV Netherlands, says Maurice Hols, channel director; 'We cater to the Dutch and Flemish part of Belgium. Both are Dutch native speakers, but we do all our communication in English because if you want to be funny or want to be cool you have to speak English; Dutch jokes are not funny! Sometimes it's a problem; a lot of Dutch viewers don't think we created the images when we produced our own idents such as "Günther" and "Brad and Eric". They think they are so good and so creative that they have come from MTV International.'

Cultural differences also mean different approaches. Obviously, individual MTV regions do not necessarily have a particularly uniform demographic structure. Even Japan, which according to Miyako Hattori, former executive producer of On-Air Promos and Creative, MTV Japan, '... is pretty much a monoculture, [has] a cultural difference between the west and east parts if you look closely'. Japan's main individuality in visual creative terms, she says, is to be seen in its lack of similarity to other cultures; 'Our culture is pretty distinctive from anywhere else; the graphics, the way we use text and the colours we choose are pretty different.'

Thus although MTV Japan has a distinctive look and feel of its own, there isn't much of a need to address different audiences within it. This is not so with MTV Latin America. Alejandro Abramovich, director of On-Air MTV Networks Latin America says he has two channels to cater to audiences that are as alike as chalk and cheese; 'Latin America is a continent with many different cultures. Our two main markets are Argentina and Mexico. Both those countries are culturally so different, almost opposites, in terms of what's cool and what's not. Being a huge brand from the United States, MTV is seen in two ways in Latin America. It's a love-hate relationship. Middle-class Mexicans look to the USA in an aspirational way. Mexico has three times the population of Argentina, only the upper-class has cable and most of them get to travel to the States frequently. In Argentina, more than fifty percent of the population has cable, they don't travel much, have lots of high quality pro-action, artistic local television and they don't look up to anything coming from the outside. In Argentina if you do something very conceptual but raw in presentation and on a low budget, they'll like it, if they like the concept. In Mexico, if it's low budget they're going to hate it, whatever the concept is.'

The result? MTV Latin America has two different channels and in terms of ident commissioning, Abramovich says he takes care to create messages with two sides; 'I might do two different idents if I'm doing a campaign spot. I will try to accomplish it without alienating anyone. For example, we have this ident where the message for Argentina is "MTV is Music", and for Mexico, "MTV is Youth". What I did is to put both messages in the one single ident, but I placed a youth concept on top and music concept a little behind.'

National or ethnic identity is certainly very much an issue in the global village these days. It seems that the more regions MTV divides into, the more potential regions and interest groups want an MTV voice of their own. MTV Nordic has recently split into four channels catering individually to Finland, Sweden, Denmark and Norway, each with their own local language. Lars Beckung, creative director, MTV Nordic, likens the Scandinavians to identical siblings; 'One thing you can say about Nordic countries is that they are very similar but they don't really want to be perceived as similar.'

Nevertheless, Beckung believes that internationality needs to remain an important aspect of the individual Nordic channels; 'People in our region feel fascinated by everything British and American. Like the Netherlands, we are small countries but British and American culture is very close to us.'

The increased need for regional flavour is also reflected in MTV Networks Asia says Charmaine Choo; 'Right now we have eighty percent international and 20% local programming'. Over the next year or so they are aiming to change that to 'sixty international and forty local', and that includes 'everything from music to promos'.

The popularity of new channels aimed at specific groups, such as MTV Desi for Indian Americans launched as part of MTV World in the USA in 2005, seems to bear out the sense of strong demand. But Cyrus Oshidar believes that too much local flavour can end in chaos; 'I think it's better to see the audience as homogenous, in India you'd go bonkers if you'd try to speak to each individual group, so we aim for the middle and go for the best.'

There could be concern that all this regional division will dilute the brand, that MTV will divide itself out of an identity and end up evolving into a whole variety of different and dissimilar entities, that bear little or no resemblance to the original parent. But in this networked era when global increasingly comes to mean uniformity, there is a far greater danger that we are slowly turning ourselves into one huge monoculture. The desire to be different, to be individual and unique is strong, and viewers look to MTV to underline and support their difference as much as helping them feel part of the MTV community. Divide and survive has to be the way ahead, but retaining those 'little spaces' on each of the myriad channels where MTV's creative identity is reinforced becomes paramount; in whichever language it is delivered.

ATTITUDE: 'Being creative makes me feel good and besides that it earns me a living.'
LOCATION: Berlin, Germany
CLIENTS: MTV, some German movie theatres, some German radio stations

MTV HEAD OF ON AIR: Thomas Sabel
DIRECTOR, CAMERA: Bettina Vogel
CAMERA: Benjamin Brettschneider
SOUND DESIGN: Jim Griffin/Zoo Studios
VOICE OVER ARTIST: Stefan Boje

CONCEPT

'This job was commissioned directly by MTV. The brief was to develop a spot or campaign that drew attention to the MTV programming around New Year 2002/2003. Apart from that, there were no restrictions whatsoever, which was nice because it left a lot of room for ideas. A few weeks earlier a friend, Benjamin Brettschneider, and I were testing out my Mini DV camera, which had a bunch of mostly useless but funny in-camera features. One of them was a mirror effect and used on human faces the result looked quite interesting. The only light in the room was an Ikea floor lamp and it turned out that this dim light gave the shots a really nice look, like a painting that I loved. When I got the New Year Campaign job, I wanted to have something strange. I remembered the faces that had been created in the Mini DV camera a few weeks earlier and decided to base the spots on them. I made six clips with six different faces.'

MAKING IT

'Actually the spots didn't take long to make. I asked some friends if they would model for me. The Mini DV camera, my friends, myself and the Ikea lamp spent one evening together and the shoot was done. The biggest problem was that they had to stay really still to make the shots work because the slightest head movement destroyed the illusion. You can see that this happened in a few moments. Since all the effects were done in-camera, there was not much post-production involved. I did not even do much grading since the look of the spots was mostly created by the lamplight. I only added the lines with the tune-in times in After Effects. Then I went to a sound studio, and without the work of the sound engineer, Jim Griffin, I think the spots would not have been as effective.

ON AIR

'The spots were produced for MTV Central and the feedback was very satisfying. Working for MTV can be quite chaotic, but you have quite a large amount of freedom. For programme-related items there is just a small bunch of people you have to present your idea to. Most of the time you only have to discuss it with the creative director, who is usually open to all kind of ideas. For this piece there were no restrictions placed on me.'

INSTRUMENT BREAK SERIES, MTV ART BREAKS

REGION

MTV INTERNATIONAL

ARTIST

SUPER2000

ATTITUDE: 'More questions, less answers.'
LOCATION: Cologne, Germany
CLIENTS: MTV International

CREDITS

MTV CREATIVE DIRECTOR: Cristian Jofre
DIRECTOR: SUPER2000
MADE BY: Manuel Hernandez, Sascha
Koeth, Jan Litzinger, Frank Zerban

CONCEPT

'Last year MTV International announced a revival of the MTV Art Breaks, which were a major trademark for MTV during the 1980s. SUPER2000 was asked to present concepts and Instrument Breaks was chosen. MTV never interfered in the conceptual process or in the production, since the Art Breaks were meant to be art and not commercials. In September 2004 we shot 19 Instrument Breaks in Cologne and did the frame-by-frame compositing one week later. All the Instrument Breaks are screened by MTV stations all over the world as bumpers between programmes, commercials and video clips.'

MAKING IT

'The production in Cologne took us three days of shooting. The performers were picked from the street, spontaneously, so the authenticity of each character could be guaranteed. Thanks to Music Store, Cologne we were supplied with a pile of musical instruments, some broken, some used, most brand new. During the production nobody got injured, except a few guitars.'

ON AIR

'Since the Instrument Breaks have been on air, we have had some very positive feedback from all over the place. Sure, there were some people who were really upset by the destruction and violence shown in the clips. But since we won a Golden Cube at the ADC Global awards, even our parents love breaking instruments.'

COUNTRYSIDE

MTV EMERGING MARKETS

KAM BHOGAL, NEIL CARTER

ATTITUDE: 'Being inspired by all aspects of life.'
LOCATION: London, UK
CLIENTS: MTV, O2, Garrards Jewellers, Straight No Chaser, Channel 4

MTV HEAD OF PROGRAMMING AND
PRODUCTION: Tanja Flintoff
DIRECTORS, IDEA, CONCEPT:
Kam Bhogal, Neil Carter
LANDSCAPE, COUNTRYSIDE DIRECTOR:
Neil Carter

CHANNEL IDENT_COUNTRYSIDE_PART FOUR OF FOUR

CONCEPT

'The idea for this clip was to present MTV not as a television channel but as an environmental experience, and help them to associate with it as one would with any cool, beautiful environment. Cool young people feature in a variety of different environments; the countryside, the city and a hair salon. Each of these settings determines an activity, such as hiking through the country, walking on the street or having a haircut. The sounds from each of the environments, birds singing, scissors snipping, cars hooting, are gradually introduced and eventually become a piece of music reflective of that particular place. For the countryside the music is mellow and ambient, for the hairsalon it is uplifting pop and for the city it's industrial house. The music combines with the beautiful visuals to create the environmental experience. The MTV logo was formed out of abstract shafts of light or shadows, making it an integral part of the surroundings.'

MAKING IT

'The piece was part of a larger commission to re-design the channel look for MTV Europe. The re-design took four months and ranged from designing navigation elements for the on-screen look to channel idents and a website re-design. The challenges on this project lay in the budget restrictions and also in the development of an idea that transcended European language barriers, as well as the creation of a new look for MTV that was fresh and progressive.
Kam Bhogal designed and developed the ideas for the environmental channel campaign, which included animated idents and on-screen identity. Kam also developed the ongoing identity for MTV Europe and the associated regions (France, NL,

Nordic, Euro) from 1999 until 2003. Neil Carter was the director of the Landscape, Urban and Hairsalon idents and also developed the environmental channel campaign; he worked at MTV from 2001 until 2003.'

ON AIR

'We gained experience in how to develop an idea for a variety of regions because the idents were not edited separately for the individual regions. They were in-house commissions from the head of MTV Europe On-Air. The content had to reflect a young demographic. The idents were filmed in the outskirts of London and could not look like they were filmed in a typical London location because they had to appeal to a European audience.'

TITLE

MTV CENTRAL CHANNEL IDENTITY 2003, BREAK BUMPERS

REGION

MTV CENTRAL

ARTIST

TANJA ADAMIETZ

ATTITUDE: 'Being creative is essential for me; it is part of myself.'
LOCATION: London, UK
CLIENTS: AOK, Armani, BBC, Campari, Lipton, MTV, Nike, Sony Ericsson, Staying Alive, Warsteiner

CREDITS

MTV HEAD OF ON AIR: Thomas Sabel
DIRECTOR: Tanja Adamietz
MTV TEAM: Thomas Sabel, Hagen Biewer, Thomas Flohr, Tina Vogel, Tim Goode, Karin Bauernfeind, Jens Bruhn
SOUND: Soho Studios, London
AVID: Frontline, London
PRODUCTION: Vis-A-Vis, Berlin

CONCEPT

'The spots were part of a series of advertising break bumpers and idents for the channel identity of MTV Central in 2003/2004. The whole series consisted of approximately 30 spots. Our idea was to combine a warm and everyday situation with something edgy and quirky. "Get inspired by MTV for every day's little craziness". How can music influence your daily life? What if your life is a record and we play it? We scratch it? The technique of scratching records inspired us to do the same with moving images. Playing scenes backwards and forwards, time mapping, stop frames and repeating frames gave the sequences an additional layer. The scratching technique added an entirely new dimension to the existing footage.'

MAKING IT

'We shot for four days in Berlin on 16mm. The very vibrant colours were achieved through the Telecine process. Before editing, all the sound was laid back on the original footage and additional sound effects were added. The scratching process was a combination of After Effects animation and Avid editing and we used different techniques, like repeating a series of frames, stopping them, playing them backwards and forwards, time mapping frames. The sound underwent the same process to make sure it fitted. Where necessary we added additional sound effects.'

ON AIR

'These clips got played a minimum of three times every hour, 24 hours a day, seven days a week, four weeks a month, 12 months a year for over a year. They were everywhere. We got great feedback and a lot of other MTV channels started playing the clips as well; even adapting the whole series as their

own channel identity. As our approach was such a simple and powerful interpretation of MTV's soul, this worked for different cultures, regions and languages.'

REGION

MTV BRAZIL

ARTIST

LOBO

ATTITUDE: 'The constant objective of doing unique work every time around.'
LOCATION: São Paulo, Brazil
CLIENTS: Viva, Diesel, Panasonic, Sony Playstation, Boomerang Channel, Gessy-Lever, Toyota, Subaru, Cartoon Network, AnimeChannel, OLN, CMT, KesselsKramer, McCann Erickson, AMC, Ogilvy & Mather Worldwide, Saatchi & Saatchi, BBDO, MTV, Disney

CREDITS

MTV PROMO MANAGER: Rodrigo Pimenta
DESIGN AND ANIMATION:
Mateus de Paula Santos, Carlos Bêla, Denis Kamioka

CONCEPT

'This was an opening for a show that featured the worst music videos of all time. "Piores Clipes" means "Worst Videos". The tough part was to suggest bad taste and relate to that, without actually making a bad taste piece, at least not 100% bad. It was also a challenge to do a funny spot. It's quite hard to do humour with motion graphics, especially in 15 seconds. The concept was to have an old golfer giving instructions on how to make a music video. We wanted something that was the exact opposite of what MTV is about. A man outside the age range of MTV's audience, playing golf, which is a sport very far from what you'd expect from the channel. This character is the most unlikely music video teacher, but that's what he's doing in the piece. What was also interesting was that it is an opening that has a host presenting the theme, not like the usual eye candy, but more like a pocketsized show. For this job we had the chance to explore a bunch of cheesy effects that we have never used since and will never use again. It was an unique opportunity.'

MITOS URBANOS, NUEVOS EPISODIOS

MTV LATIN AMERICA

TREVOR LAFARGUE

ATTITUDE: 'Always have fun; if you are not having fun, then its work.'
LOCATION: Miami, USA
CLIENTS: MTV Latin America

MTV DIRECTOR, ON AIR:
Alejandro Abramovich
DIRECTOR: Trevor Lafargue
ASSOCIATE PRODUCER:
Santiago Andrade

CONCEPT

'This was a promo featuring new episodes of "The Urban Myth Show" in our prime-time block called "L'Güeveo". As producers at MTV we get weekly assignments from our programming strategy. We took the ideas from tabloid magazines that sensationalise myths. Anyone who stands too long in a check-out line in the grocery store ends up reading the crazy headlines from the tabloid magazines. That's how this idea came up, standing in line at the store. We chose to use local Latin American myths like "el Chupacabra", and well-known myths such as vampires and exploding implants after plastic surgery. It was a lot of fun to cut and paste random images, and then go crazy with our copywriter to create a fun and attention-grabbing spot.'

MAKING IT

'The main challenge was the animation. Santiago Andrade, another producer and graphic designer, helped set the After Effects animations and keyframes. It was just a matter of having fun after that.'

ON AIR

'Feedback was great, everyone loved the spot, and thought it really caught the eye, and that was the point; to get your attention and make you watch the new episodes. There were some restrictions; we wanted to show an old photo of a painting of a woman showing her breasts. We had a part in the script where we mentioned the myth of implants exploding after plastic surgery, but we were unable to show it, due to censorship.'

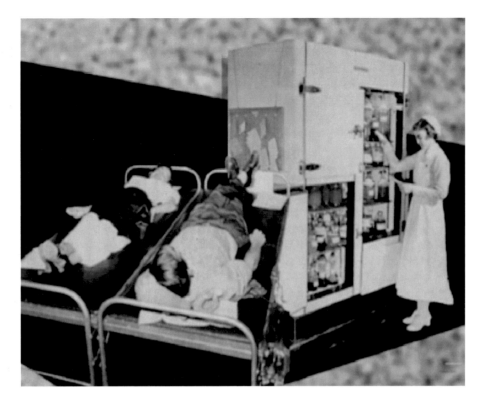

Un ejército de vampiros busca donantes de sangre para un hospital.

CIERTO

FALSO

INFERNO II:
THE GOOD GUYS VS.
THE BAD ASSES,
TONYA AND GIRLFIGHT

REGION

MTV US

ARTIST

FREESTYLE COLLECTIVE

ATTITUDE: 'Having a pen, camera or mouse in our hands is as natural to us as a bird taking flight. Our mantra is; Freedom to Think, Create, and Design'
LOCATION: New York, USA
CLIENTS: MTV, VH1, Saatchi & Saatchi, Fuel Network, Cartoon Network, Bravo, Ogilvy, Comedy Central, Young & Rubicam, Showtime, Fallon Advertising

CREDITS

MTV SVP ON AIR DESIGN AND OFF AIR:
Jeffrey Keyton
MTV SVP ON AIR PROMOS: Kevin Mackall
CREATIVE DIRECTOR: Victor Newman
EXECUTIVE PRODUCER:
Suzanne Potashnick
DESIGNER, ANIMATOR: Brian Sensebe
ANIMATOR: Ken Tanabe
3D ANIMATOR: Entae Kim
AUDIO: Hot Head Music
VOICE OVER: Todd Horman,
Pialo Hertz, Shannon Mattaro

CONCEPT

'Freestyle Collective collaborated with MTV on a promo graphics package for the second season of the competition-driven show "The Inferno". Past participants of the shows "Road Rules" and "The Real World" battle it out in a series of challenges to win bragging rights and a cash prize of $300,000. The creative brief from MTV stated that the theme of the promo campaign should be derived from comic book. The Freestyle Collective, being very familiar with comic books and all the styles associated with them, was glad to take on the challenge.'

MAKING IT

'The challenge was to create an animated comic book environment with dimension and depth. The team had to focus on highlighting the talent from the show while allowing the viewer to feel as if they were travelling seamlessly through the pages of "The Inferno II" comic book. Once the storyboard had been approved by MTV we began production by mapping out the path of the journey into the environment. We then referenced photographs of the talent and illustrated all of them in Vector Form in order not to lose any resolution. The two teams the "Good Guys" and the "Bad Asses" were illustrated to reflect their character and group affiliation.'

ON AIR

'The great script writing for "The Inferno II" project gave us a lot of comic situations to animate. We can't help but laugh when these spots are shown. They were created for the US market.'

BEAT EATER

MTV US

TODD ST. JOHN / HUNTERGATHERER

LOCATION: New York, USA
CLIENTS: MTV, VH1, Sundance, Nixon, Nike, Surfing, Burton, New York Times, Fuse, 2K

CREDITS

MTV SVP ON AIR DESIGN AND OFF AIR: Jeffrey Keyton
MTV SVP ON AIR PROMOS: Kevin Mackall
DIRECTOR, DESIGNER: Todd St. John
ANIMATORS: Fabian Tejada, Christopher Gereg, Todd St. John
MUSIC: Adam Rourke

CONCEPT

'This was are a series of three clips created for MTV2; Breaker, Ukulele and Sax. Each was done to a brief about music. The concept for each centres around a creature that gets excited when exposed to music, to the point that he's compelled to literally consume it, in each case eating the person or thing making the music. In doing so, he destroys the music-maker, but assumes a few of their characteristics, he changes colour to match them, for example.'

MAKING IT

'It was a small project and there wasn't a huge animation budget, so it was created fairly quickly. I wanted it to be very simple in animation style, a stop-motion, cut-paper kind of look. In the end it was all done digitally, with some physical elements incorporated into it.'

ON AIR

'Generally speaking, when working for MTV, the feedback is more upfront, in saying "yes" or "no" to the idea. I think I've done enough projects with them (and worked as an art director there for a time) that once the idea is given the go-ahead, they usually let me execute it without much outside direction.'

TITLE

LE RÉGULATEUR,
LE PROCESSUS,
MTV ART BREAKS

REGION

MTV INTERNATIONAL

ARTIST

PHILIPPE GRAMMATICOPOULOS

ATTITUDE: 'Constructing an original graphic and narrative world.'
LOCATION: Paris, France
CLIENTS: Le Monde, Arte, Centre Georges Pompidou, Storyboard, Etapes Graphiques, Res magazine, Repérages, Sonovision

CREDITS

MTV CREATIVE DIRECTOR: Cristian Jofre
DIRECTOR: Philippe Grammaticopoulos
3D TEAM: Christophe Barnouin,
Nicolas Combecave, Thibaud Deloof,
Philippe Grammaticopoulos,
Xavier de l'Hermuzière, David Liébard,
Lucas Vallerie, Baptiste Van Opstal
MUSIC: Marc Delouvrier

CONCEPT

'I like universal themes, science is one of them, with its investigations, its discoveries, the hope it brings for all of us and also the ethical problems it brings up. The media often speak about bioethics and cloning. I took that as my starting point for my movie Le Régulateur, and I imagined how it would be, in a near future, if human reproduction became industrialised and turned into mass production. I created a factory where couples could choose their child, like going shopping in the supermarket. The other theme I tackle with Le Processus is social exclusion. I chose some excerpts from these two movies for the MTV Art Breaks project. I edited them anew and made an original soundtrack.'

MAKING IT

'I make my 3D movies with the computer. I'm still very close to my 2D habits, which is why I try to flatten the 3D, bringing together background and form, using the light, the frontal centring and the utilisation of long focal length. That is the main challenge. I try to take the opposite view of classic 3D iconography, to make movies that do not appear to be either 3D or 2D, but a blend of both.'

ON AIR

'This work has been very important for me because of the broad distribution of the Art Breaks all over the world. MTV has contacted me regarding for a new project and I hope to work for them again. The only restriction was to include an MTV logo in the clip; apart from that MTV gives the artist a lot of freedom, which is very pleasant.'

SWARM, MTV ART BREAKS

MTV INTERNATIONAL

JOHN-PAUL HARNEY

ATTITUDE: 'It is always important to me to keep away from becoming too didactic.'
LOCATION: London, UK
CLIENTS: National Geographic Channel, Schweppes, Ford, Vodaphone, Goldfish, Rover, BMW, MTV

MTV CREATIVE DIRECTOR: Cristian Jofre
DIRECTOR: John-Paul Harney

CONCEPT

'We see a head chomping away greedily, a grasping hand ripping wheat from the ground and the animal stuffing his face as we pull out to reveal a horde of locusts with human heads in an insatiable feeding frenzy. The swarm flies off leaving a decimated field to move on to a pasture of lush green vegetation, their next victim. The concept for Swarm is based on issues of sustainable development and mankind's consumption of natural and finite resources. It was an idea that was part of a suite of three short pieces I had planned a couple of years previously but which had to be shelved in favour of a much larger project at the time. When Peter Moller called about the new series of Art Breaks it seemed a good opportunity to resurrect it. It is a short piece intended to get across a simple idea; that man cannot go on unchecked and not expect to eventually find himself in a barren landscape, which can no longer support him. So I have embodied him as a human locust. It is important to me to keep away from becoming too didactic. I've seen far too many pieces which come across as thou shalt and thou shalt not that often turns me off any cause. Often, humour can be used as the spoonful of sugar to help the medicine go down but in this case I wanted a darker feel more like the realm of Hieronymus Bosch, so I chose to create a very stylistic piece.'

MAKING IT

'Visually the aesthetic is of a crosshatched ink drawing with washes of colour. Like the drawings by John Tenniel for the "Alice in Wonderland" and "Through the Looking Glass" books by Lewis Carroll, which suit the surrealist nature of the piece. There are three basic washes of colour over the drawing, which are applied in a very haphazard fashion, as though the person painting is in a hurry to get their task done, which fits with the frantic behaviour of the locusts but is in contrast to the very methodical nature of the drawing and shading. It was executed using Softimage XSI, a 3D application used on many of today's effects-laden films. My main task was to develop a rendering method that has all the feel of a hand-made piece, but without the prohibitive production overheads. Actually drawing, shading and colouring the film would have taken months and a great deal of my sanity; as an animator I don't have that much patience.'

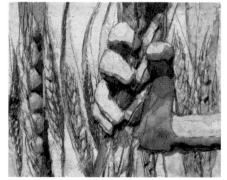

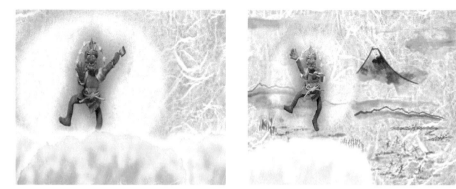

RAIN GOD

MTV ASIA

FUMI INOUE

ATTITUDE: 'In a busy world, we tend to miss small precious moments which exist right next to us. I love to show those things to others through my creativity and vision.'
LOCATION: Tokyo, Japan

MTV DIRECTOR, ON AIR PROMOTIONS, CREATIVE AND CONTENT: Charmaine Choo
DIRECTOR: Fumi Inoue

CONCEPT

'Studying abroad at the National Film and Television School encouraged me to look back at my roots. The chance discovery of using Japanese paper, blots of ink and the texture of torn paper stimulated my imagination to make this work. This project was actually an exercise I'd done for college. I had made another film that I pitched to MTV, but they asked me to send all my previous school projects and they finally ended up selecting this one. I was given the sound first to make an animation to music as an exercise in college. The sound, especially the drum, inspired me to depict the ceremony of praying for rain.'

MAKING IT

'My main goal during my time at college was searching for more ways of making model animation. The digital tool saved me from the restriction of camera work. I had two months to finish the whole project. The main problem was that I had to do it all by myself, the figure of Rain God as well as the filming.'

ON AIR

'MTV is a globally famous company and that credit helps me to impress passionate people.'

RAIN GOD

TITLE

GIANTS,
MTV ART BREAKS

REGION

MTV INTERNATIONAL

ARTIST

WOUTER SEL

ATTITUDE: 'What I am aiming for is that you can actually believe what is on the screen.'
LOCATION: Gent, Belgium
CLIENTS: MTV

CREDITS

MTV CREATIVE DIRECTOR: Cristian Jofre
CONCEPT, DESIGN, STORYBOARD,
ANIMATION COMPOSITING,
POST-PRODUCTION: Wouter Sel
SOUND DESIGN: Pieter Van Houte

CONCEPT

'The rough idea for Giants was conceived in one of my sketchbooks. It was a silly drawing, with little meaning. When Peter Moller from MTV asked me for treatments for the Art Breaks, I immediately thought of that drawing, and made up a story behind it. What were these giants doing? And why? The pay-off of this mini-story is as minimal as it is simple: these three creatures have lost their giant kitty, and they are calling it back. I still have to complete the fourth episode where they are reunited. Perhaps for the next Art Breaks project?'

MAKING IT

'The main challenge was timing. It was difficult to make the episodes look very slow and static in a short amount of time. My goal was that people would think that these creatures have been standing there for ages, calling for something that wouldn't come. And the giant cat should look as if it had been on the road for years. I've also tried to create genuine relationships between the giants. I looked at them as three brothers; the one in the middle being the eldest and a bit passive, the right one as the middle brother who's a bit dominant and the left one the youngest, a little playful, and not that bright. And it's his cat that is missing. I actually don't mind if people don't get these storylines. It's not that important for the audience, but it is for me, since I believe you can feel it, rather than see it, and that is what I am aiming for; that you can actually believe what is on the screen, absurd as it may be. Pieter Van Houte did an excellent job on the sound design. He sure couldn't do much with my pointers. How do you explain that these things are supposed to make a sound that no human can produce? We had lots of fun though, and he gave me just what the clip needed and more. All in all the clips took

four weeks to make. The hardest part was deciding what was necessary, and leaving everything out that wasn't essential.'

ON AIR

'Although one of the episodes of Giants was selected for a Promax-award for Best On-Air Branding, and I have received numerous compliments on my work, I can't really say that these clips have had professional results yet. But since animation is a tricky professional world, I don't worry about this. It's there on my resumé, anyway. The best part is that I got to make these clips, and that I'm proud of the result. Having MTV in my portfolio is amazing, of course, and I am sure that it'll work to my advantage. I was told that this was a project for MTV worldwide, and that different MTV regions were free to air the clips they wanted. Living in Belgium, I've only seen mine aired twice, but it's an amazing feeling knowing that they may be aired in Guatamala or Nepal or anywhere you can imagine. All in all, I'd do it again in a second.'

STAYING AHEAD

SOPHIE LOVELL

Maintaining freshness, being different, inspiring and creative has always been a major priority at MTV, even if there are significant moments when the business side of being a multinational corporation looks in danger of taking over.

It is not only the input from external creatives, animators, film and video makers that helps to keep the channel on the cutting edge, it is also all the creative directors who commission them, both regionally and from the umbrella creative department at MTV International. These are the people charged with the care and development of the brand's visual identity, and they are the ones who steer a course, between the tastes and customs of their viewers and the creative capacity of their artists, into the wide blue yonder.

'There's lots of things that contribute towards making a channel identity', says Cam Levin, vice president, Creative, MTV Networks International. *'It's about building an image that is a generic message about the channel as a whole. An ident is part of this identity system, which is everything from how the logo looks in the top corner of the screen to the way you title your music videos, and the way you menu your channel. It all goes towards the look and feel or perception of the channel. The ident itself is a chance to punctuate each hour or 20 minutes after an ad break and put a signature to the channel, so as to remind viewers of which channel they are watching. It will also re-instate your ethos or whatever it is you want to get across.'*

Idents, those little snippets of moving graphics or very short films, often only a few seconds long, that end in the MTV logo, are key to the channel.

'The unique thing at MTV is that you can immediately tell it's the channel when you're channel surfing because of the graphics', says Lars Beckung, creative director at MTV Nordic. From the start, by positioning itself as a music platform made by rock 'n' rollers with crazy left-field attitudes, MTV found a way of incorporating experimental animation and graphics into the very fabric of itself. Now, 25 years on, this sense of need and duty to be visually inspirational is a firmly engrained company ethos.

Idents tend to take two forms; there are the channel idents that are part of the graphic look of the channel, and there are the Art Breaks, which are longer but not specifically about any particular event or part of the channel, simply little pieces of art between the programming. *'They are more about MTV's brand values'*, says Cam Levin, *'to support artists and showcase more creative bits of animation.'* The Art Breaks may be strange, weird, confrontational, happy, sad, whatever and in all manner of media. The only thing they have in common is the MTV logo at the end which says; 'This fascinating, strange, inspiring little artwork was not only brought to you by MTV it is MTV'. The idents make MTV cool and MTV makes the idents cool. It is a curious, symbiotic relationship.

In the early days, idents and channel graphics were concerned with one identity. Now they have to say; 'You are watching MTV'; as well as telling the viewer which particular one of the forty-odd MTV channels they are watching. The rules of branding are not carved in stone at MTV, each region has their own individual approach and it's more about reflecting the spirit of the company. Cyrus Oshidar, senior vice president, Creative and Content, MTV India describes his region's attitude; *'MTV India doesn't have a style guide. We refer to our style as a "bhel buri". That's a dish with mixed tastes and flavours; it's brasher, louder, faster, bigger, better. Our graphics are designed to be imperfect because that's what India is. If the logo falls off at some point during the promo then so be it.'*

Part of being innovative is the ability to be fast and flexible when it comes to bringing a new look to the channel. The process between conception and on-air needs to be extremely fast. If the end result work then it can come off again just as quickly.

'In the UK', says Georgia Cooke, head of UK On-Air, MTV UK, *'we like to give something like an*

image campaign four to six weeks lead time. That gives everybody time to get the creative elements right. Obviously if it is time-reactive then we are talking about one to two weeks'.

Most MTV regions say that producing new creative stuff quickly is not the difficult part, it is the quantity and available manpower that cause the limitations. Georgia Cooke agrees; *'We are a very small department with only five creatives to cover all five UK channels, so the difficulty we have is due to the number of projects we can process at any one time. We often have up to 50 live projects, from a promo to a bit of graphics or channel redesigns. Sometimes we can be working on three channel redesigns at once. It's great but it means we never ever put the brakes on, we are always going at a thousand miles an hour; although we have loads of ideas we sometimes can't do what we would like to do, which is a real shame.'*

A part of staying ahead also means that regions tend to pay a lot of attention to youth trends. In the UK, according to Georgia Cooke, they have a *'very active research department who do a lot of qualitative research into our audience and their belief systems, attitudes and what they are consuming'.* MTV Nordic too, says Lars Beckung, spends a lot of time and energy on research; *'It's important for people working with the brand and also it's one of our selling points for our clients; being a youth expert is an important part of our USP.'*

But Maurice Hols, channel director, MTV Netherlands takes a completely opposite approach; *'We believe in our own trends. We don't use hip people and we don't believe in trendy people. Our attitude is that even if you just take a carton of milk and put our logo on it, then the milk becomes sexy. Or like the car brand Lada, for example, it's not sexy, but I bought three Lada Nivas for my presenters and had them painted in three different colours: a pink one, one with flames and one with stars. We now use them as company cars or for events. So that's what we can do; take a non-sexy brand like Lada and make it cool. Right now every car brand is calling me and wants to work with MTV. That's the way we do it.'*

Approaches also vary when it comes to scouting for new talent to generate new graphics and idents. Whereas Japan, for example, might have a department with three employees delivering regular weekly scouting reports, MTV South's former vice president, creative director Maurizio Vitale prefers a more relaxed networking attitude; *'Once in a while someone comes up from the On-Air department and says "Hey, I met this photographer and she's really nice and could do a piece for us with pictures, do you want to see her?" It is very informal.'*

In a way it is quite easy to be relatively informal and collect intelligence by word of mouth, Internet research or reading magazines and generally staying in touch with other creative departments around at MTV, says Georgia Cooke, because *'MTV is just an extraordinary creative community and probably the only one that is this sophisticated in the world'.* In other words the whole company is a magnet for creative ideas.

Nevertheless MTV cannot afford to sit back and wait for fresh talent to come walking through its doors. Fresh talent is the creative life-blood of the company, without it MTV is no different from all the rest. Cam Levin; *'We prefer to use new and untried people and design houses because we constantly want to keep it fresh and re-invent ourselves, rock the boat and question the status quo.'*

True, people often send films and designs in on spec (some even have the MTV logo) but generally it is the On-Air departments of each region that collect and filter new work, and this often means holding competitions, and collaborating with art colleges. Some creative directors also see it as their duty to support and nurture young designers and design education. Lars Beckung is proud of this part of his work; *'We do mid and end term projects with art schools, it's a great way of keeping close to the next trends. And once they're finished studying we keep working with them. We build up a good relationship. It's a long-standing tradition.'*

Working with students or giving young designers their first break often brings up the question of whether MTV is exploiting young people's ideas, by paying them far less than they might have to dish out to an established company. It is an issue that Cam Levin feels strongly about:

'I think it is more about giving someone a platform that they wouldn't normally have to show their work; and there is a real win-win relationship going on. Obviously, MTV gets to tap into some new talent and get some exciting material onto the channels, but by the same token this person will also get massive exposure. It's a great thing for their showreel. There will be contacts made through the work that they have done for MTV that will take them to another level, and perhaps into a broader working space.'

Of course MTV does not rely on students and graduates for its entire creative output. Established design companies are often used, especially for a big job that requires reliability and experience, such as a new channel identity. MTV Netherlands relies almost exclusively on the creative company John Doe for new idents and visuals (they regularly produce around 10 pieces per year for MTV) and it has turned out to be a very fruitful partnership. Others, like MTV India, rely predominantly on their own in-house team when it comes to ident production. Charmaine Choo, director, On-Air promotions MTV Networks Asia tends to choose individuals over companies, if she can, for creative work; *'Sometimes it's nicer to work with freelancers because they're hungrier for it. I've had some not so positive experiences when we've paid a well known motion graphics company, and the results have been less exciting because they haven't got the passion.'*

Budget is also a major decider in whether to use a young, untried talent or a design house for a commission. Budgets for creative projects vary enormously, from practically zero for an in-house 'Mac' production to hundreds of thousands of Euros for a big music awards promo campaign.

Finally, it is important to note the enormous effects that technical innovations have had on the style and content of both creative input and output at MTV. Production and post-production, for example, have been completely revolutionised.

Whereas, just a few years ago, MTV would have to spend thousands of Euros on specialist technicians and equipment to create effects, today most requirements are met in-house with After Effects or Final Cut Pro software and a powerful Mac.

As a result, new work submitted by students and designers is also on the increase, says Cam Levin; *'If you had wanted to make films before you would have had to go to film school and learn to edit with the old splicing techniques; now you've got software on a home computer that can do pretty much what they were doing in big post-production houses five or ten years ago. Everyone's filming their birthday or their ski trip, everyone's doing a little music and adding their graphics to it or animating with Flash for the web. All these bits of software have made what used to be only for professionals available to people at home on their laptops. This has meant that a lot more people are experimenting; a lot more people are trying out their creativity, even if it is only to make something to send to their friends.'*

Experimental film-making and animation has become faster, cheaper, easier, more accessible and more compatible. One would think that this would be reflected in a blaze of increased creative activity on the MTV channels. There is an awful lot more of it around to choose from, says Maurice Hols wryly, *'but that does not mean that the stuff you get sent is necessarily any good'.*

ORIGAMI, MTV ART BREAKS

MTV INTERNATIONAL

THOMAS HILLAND / PARTIZAN

LOCATION: London, UK
CLIENTS: Diesel Clothing, Sony, Virgin
Music, MTV, EMI Music, Wall of Sound

MTV CREATIVE DIRECTOR: Cristian Jofre
DIRECTOR: Thomas Hilland
PRODUCER: Russel Curtis, Isabella Parish
PRODUCTION MANAGER: Pia Dueholm
DOP: Ray Coates
3D: Partizan Lab Paris
PRODUCTION CO: Partizan London
EDITOR: Sue Davis, Final Cut
MUSIC: Elektrofant

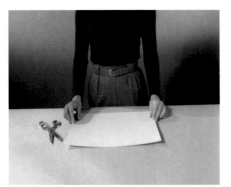

CONCEPT

'The ident was commissioned by MTV to be a part of their new batch of Art Breaks. It is inspired by children's arts and crafts programmes typical of the 1970s, where you used old toilet-rolls and scraps of paper to make Christmas presents for the whole family.'

MAKING IT

'The film involved fusing the live-action of cutting and folding paper together with computer-generated images, linking scenes of real paper with animated 3D. The main challenge was to make the 3D stuff work together with the shot footage. Plain white paper is not as easy to reproduce in a computer as one would think because the shadows, folds and bends of the paper are very varied from one angle to the next. The film took about two weeks to make. After we shot the folding process, in one day, the remaining work was in 3D. We shot the origami woman in a small studio with many different paper models made up in advance in all kinds of shapes, ranging from plain white sheets of paper to the finished MTV logo, complete with the trademark ®. This was shot on 35mm film. We had a paper model guy standing by to make shapes in case we needed some more during the shoot. The editing process was about finding the best parts, leaving blanks in between that were to be filled in by the 3D sections. Then the musicians came knocking. We missed Sunday but came up smiling Monday.'

ON AIR

'The MTV project was interesting as the brief was completely open, which is any film-maker's dream scenario.'

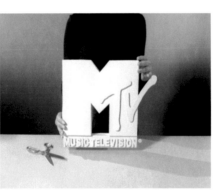

MTV LIEBT GÜNTHER

MTV EUROPE

JOHN DOE AMSTERDAM

ATTITUDE: 'John Doe's mission is to deconstruct the whole world and make it into a pill so that we can swallow it with a cool beer at the end of time. Our mission is to spend our time on this planet with good people and good ideas and not the other way round.'
LOCATION: Amsterdam, the Netherlands
CLIENTS: MTV, Bacardi, Lada, Tetra Pak, Johan magazine, City Council Rotterdam, Martini

MTV HEAD OF ON AIR: Thomas Sabel
AGENCY: John Doe Amsterdam
ART DIRECTOR: Hein Mevissen
COPYWRITER: Diederiekje Bok,
Rob Doubal
DIRECTOR: Steve Ayson
PRODUCTION COMPANY:
The Sweetshop New Zealand
DOP: Jaq Fitzgerald
EDITOR: Sam Brunette
POST PRODUCTION:
Oktobor, Valkieser Capital Images
SOUND: Studio de Keuken

CONCEPT

'Günther was born in a bar when a John Doe member recounted the story of a great uncle who, after the war, had hidden his German roots from his grandchildren to save them the embarrassment associated with wartime Germany. It seemed a difficult way of solving his identity crisis, therefore John Doe imagined an alternative approach. An approach that both John Doe and MTV would be proud of; he would confess to his family. To emphasize the catharsis, Günther would be black, and live with his white middle class parents. MTV loves Günther because he is not ashamed to admit who he really is and gets on with it. He is representative of all people who are honest, confident and progressive. In a world that easily conforms, MTV and John Doe want to inspire new leaders who will take us to new and better places.'

MAKING IT

'The shoot took place in New Zealand using 35mm film. The filming was very interesting because everybody who worked on this shoot also worked on the film "Lord of the Rings". Our DOP was the first assistant cameraman for "Lord of the Rings". The light in New Zealand is really great, and totally different to that in Europe which means that you get completely different effects.'

ON AIR

'The effect of broadcasting these commercials was amazing. Günther got his own fan mail and fan websites. He also became a popular chat room topic. There was much discussion about the identity of his creators, if they were German or Swiss, Swedish or English? We notice that elements of Günther are copied by other creatives and see it as a compliment. John Doe works for MTV Benelux, but all the short

films we've made including Günther or the films called Brad and Eric (these are also really popular), were made for MTV Europe. John Doe make new short films every month and every film shows a different aspect of MTV. All the films contain humour but we avoid corny, easy, sex-related jokes.'

BLAME MTV

MTV US

DAVID HOROWITZ

ATTITUDE: 'The idea is king. I try not to rely on execution to solve what is missing in the idea.'
LOCATION: New York, USA

CREDITS

MTV SVP ON AIR DESIGN AND OFF AIR:
Jeffrey Keyton
MTV SVP ON AIR PROMOS: Kevin Mackall
WRITER, DIRECTOR: David Horowitz
PRODUCER: Jerelyn Orlandi
DOP: Paul Goldsmith
PRODUCTION DESIGNER: Susan Block
EDITOR: Nathan Byrne, Post Millennium
AUDIO: Laki Fotopoulos, Hot Head

CONCEPT

'This spot, part of a three-spot campaign called "Blame MTV", was inspired by a simple truth; MTV's influence on youth culture is unparalleled. To some that is a good thing, and to others it is a serious problem. In America today, with its fractured and reactionary political climate, everyone is trying to assign blame for the various things that are supposedly wrong with youth culture; its music, attitude, etc. Since MTV is the place that most connect with the real youth experience, I thought it was about time we got some of that well-deserved blame ourselves (tongue firmly in cheek, of course). So this spot was a way of comically and defiantly acknowledging that it is MTV's fault and we take full responsibility. At the time, I noticed a proliferation of little girls singing like they were Whitney Houston. The vocal gymnastics trend, personified by Christina Aguilera, was everywhere, which is what sparked this particular idea. How far into American life had MTV caused this to seep? This spot was a comic answer to that question.'

MAKING IT

'The most important element in the production of this spot was finding the right girl. It was crucial she sing in a way that would transcend her age, that this incredible voice would be the last thing you would expect to come out of her. We auditioned a number of young girls, many with Broadway experience, looking for one who had the perfect mix of awkwardness and vocal ability. Melissa Taibi, once we heard and saw her, became the obvious choice. She had a truly amazing voice, enough so to have performed at the world-famous Apollo Theater in Harlem. Unfortunately, she had never even been to a Bat Mitzvah nor did she know much about what it was, so I worked with her to learn the

Hebrew prayer song phonetically. Not being able to write music myself, I taught her the modified diva melody by singing it to her over and over again, scribbling out the roller coaster vocal pattern as a series of squiggly lines. We shot the spot on 16mm film in one day on location outside New York City. One challenge was finding a synagogue that would allow us to shoot there. The one we wound up shooting at was very cooperative, and most of the extras were actual congregants who volunteered. This had its advantages and disadvantages, as many of them had their own, very vocal, opinions about the authenticity of my particular Bat Mitzvah scene. Overall, though, they had a good time.'

ON AIR

'One unexpected result of this clip was that various synagogues have requested copies to show their Bar and Bat Mitzvah classes as an inspirational and learning tool, which I find incredibly funny yet gratifying. Ironically, these spots were pulled from air not long after they began airing. The reason? Janet Jackson's breast. Showing her tit in the MTV produced Super Bowl half-time show caused a ridiculous, but very real, national outcry and much cultural hand-wringing. MTV came under intense scrutiny and pressure from citizen groups and the government, and fear was running rampant. Here was MTV literally being blamed for the loosening of standards in American society, the cause of all

that is wrong with the world. So MTV decided it was not wise to have a campaign on the air with the tagline "Blame MTV", which they feared would be taken as an affront in the aftermath of Janet-gate. Unbelievable. But in a way, that made the spot even more meaningful to me, since it clearly hit on a moment in the culture, of MTV at least, when such blame placing was at its peak.'

TITLE

MTV UK CHANNEL DESIGN AND IDENTS

REGION

MTV UK

ARTIST

DIXONBAXI

ATTITUDE: 'We set up dixonbaxi as a self-ish entity; to enjoy life and our work, to keep things simple, to avoid bullshit, not to lie or oversell our work. Hopefully we create well-crafted projects and are as re-laxed as possible along the way.'
LOCATION: London, UK
CLIENTS: MTV Europe, Formula 1, Viacom, O2, VH1, The Biography Channel, 3 Mobile, KultureFlash, Channel 4, RotoVision

CREDITS

MTV HEAD OF CREATIVE: Georgia Cooke
CONCEPT AND DIRECTION: dixonbaxi
PRODUCTION COMPANY: The Business
DOP: John Pardue
AUDIO: NBAW

CONCEPT

'It was our second channel design for MTV after creating MTV2. We were inspired by a brief to cap-ture creativity with a British flavour; something that would make a specific connection to UK view-ers and tap into the quirks and sensibilities of our humour and world-view. It was commissioned via the in-house creative team at MTV who worked closely with us on the tone and feel. It is part of an ongoing relationship with the MTV team we have worked with since 2001.'

MAKING IT

'We wanted to create a cast of characters that pop-ulate the MTV UK world. These became a series of short vignettes that explored the heightened real-ity of our alternative take on British Culture. Fast, weird and a little twisted, they are humorous mo-ments that pop up around the MTV programmes. We shot the idents on film over a three-day shoot and during that time wrangled with strange sets, lots of live animals and a few stuffed ones. We shot very intensively to create many variations and crafted moments. The whole set was very stylised with clear art direction and camera framing. We had pre-planned in great detail so as to capture exactly the look and feel we wanted. We learned that the old adage of, never work with children and animals is true.'

ON AIR

'Working with MTV is a real bonus. They allow lots of freedom and are very receptive to ideas. It helps dixonbaxi to avoid getting pigeonholed into a cer-tain style. We've shot live action, created illustra-tions, used pure typography, played with graph-ics, and the MTV team always look at things with a fresh pair of eyes. We don't have to repeat styles or ideas we've created before, which is good as it avoids us getting stale. It doesn't allow us to rest on our laurels because each new project is fresh and different. There is also a creative caché that comes with showing MTV work to other prospective cli-ents. It excites them and shows our work at its most eclectic. Overall MTV are looser than a lot of clients and trust us to deliver good work for them.'

GREAT ESCAPES: CAR

MTV US

TED PAULY

ATTITUDE: 'For the most part, I'm just trying to get images on MTV that have the feel of real life; funny, sad, ugly, pretty, heart-warming and irritating, often simultaneously.'
LOCATION: USA
CLIENTS: MTV

CREDITS

MTV SVP ON AIR DESIGN AND OFF AIR: Jeffrey Keyton
MTV SVP ON AIR PROMOS: Kevin Mackall
DIRECTOR: Ted Pauly
CREATIVE DIRECTOR: Kevin Mackall, MTV
DIRECTOR, WRITER: Ted Pauly, MTV
EDITOR: Brad Turner, Post Millennium
AUDIO: Laki Fotopoulos, Hothead
DOP: Terry Stacey
MUSIC: The 101

CONCEPT

'The piece was created for MTV On-Air promos, my department at work. The brief was simple; create spots that connect MTV with the younger end of its viewing audience. My idea was just that when we're teenagers, we feel trapped by a variety of things, and we're sometimes given to dramatic "Me versus The World" moments. Why not force that generalised sense of teenage persecution into an awkward monologue? In the spot called Car, there was also the added bonus of depicting that overwrought teenage drama via an awkward, low-speed car chase.'

MAKING IT

'We shot the spot in six hours, on 16mm Kodak film stock with an ARRI camera. Sound was recorded with boom and wireless to DAT. Originally, the car was supposed to be covered from a camera mounted on the hood, but the car arrived so late that we had to settle for what we could get from the side. As a result of being behind schedule, we had to rely on our young actor to get his monologue right in fewer than ten takes. I guess if I learned anything, it was a) to never count on the prop car being delivered on time, and b) that hiring a really good actor can make or break a spot like this.'

ON AIR

'I'm not sure how the spot connected with viewers, but it did get some attention from commercial production companies. MTV is the only client I know well, but my sense is that other commercial clients are much more risk-averse and into micromanagement. MTV is open to promoting itself with this less direct, soft-sell kind of branding, which is incredibly liberating from a creative standpoint.'

BARK

MTV LATIN AMERICA

MIGUEL CALDERON

ATTITUDE: 'To continue working even after failing; to achieve and learn something in the process of making.'
LOCATION: Mexico City, Mexico
CLIENTS: MTV, Andrea Rosen Gallery NY, Kurimanzutto Gallery, Mexico

MTV DIRECTOR, ON AIR:
Alejandro Abramovich
DIRECTOR: Miguel Calderon
PRODUCER: Daniela Perez
CAMERA: Tabby, Yamit
ACTORS: Mauricio Calderon, Gaba
MUSIC: Alexis Ruiz

CONCEPT

'Bark is based on a true story about a guy who went around the neighbourhood forcing people to bark at gunpoint, and once they started barking he would drive off. What inspired me? How fucked the story was. The idea evolved after one of my best friends told me that it had happened to his dad. I was curious about what drove a guy to humiliate people by making them bark so I decided that the best way to understand what had happened was by recreating it. I was thinking of integrating the idea into a screenplay I was writing or shooting it as a loop for an art show. Then MTV contacted me and asked me if I wanted to shoot some spots. I like making videos so I thought it would be nice to have people see my idea on a larger scale than in a gallery.'

MAKING IT

'The main challenge was to have the idea make sense in just one minute. It took a few hours to set the shot and about four shooting runs. There was no editing since it was all in one shot. One whole day was spent finding the location and asking the neighbours to let us use the street. We used a 16mm film camera and daylight; we borrowed a BMW from a very nice friend. The main difficulties were; having people bark at the right time and getting people in the neighbourhood to let us shoot there. After a while the residents wanted to be in the video, which was fun. Basically, all the crew were friends, and my dad who was one of the main actors and did an amazing job at barking.'

ON AIR

'Not too many people know I did it but I've heard some good reactions. Other people say that it's too aggressive. I did what I pleased for this clip, no questions asked. My clients deal directly with my gallery and buy what they like. I would totally do a spot a week if I could, since it was so much fun doing it.'

JESUS CAN'T SNEEZE

MTV UK

LESLIE ALI

ATTITUDE: 'I like to make things which haven't been made before. The goal is to make my audience feel something, react, laugh, worry, think.'
LOCATION: London, UK
CLIENTS: Nike, Coca-Cola, Doritos, The Guardian, Volkswagen, 3 (Hutchinson 3 Telecoms), Mini Cooper, MTV

MTV HEAD OF CREATIVE: Georgia Cooke
DIRECTOR: Leslie Ali
DOP: Zach Nicholson
WRITER: Leslie Ali
PRODUCER: Jacob Madsen
ACTOR: Tim Plester

CONCEPT

'The clip is part of a series of moments the bible left out; the stuff somebody forgot to write down, like the things Jesus is not so good at. The clip Sneeze is one of ten executions featured on the MTV Music Awards in 2004. I thought it'd be a bit more interesting to explore Jesus' more human side. MTV commissioned it when they saw the idea on paper. It was shot and finished for Easter, but as I understand it, a couple of the clips were considered too controversial for the holiday time slot. So instead, they ran the whole series of ten clips as bumpers for the MTV Music Awards.'

MAKING IT

'Finding Jesus was tricky. I needed a smart actor who got exactly what I was trying to do. Once I found Tim, we began developing the concept together. He makes me look good. Comedy can be tough. You've got to be brave enough to try anything and give your character the freedom to assume his natural rhythm, and be prepared to evolve his interpretation. Experimentation is key; as is timing. It's painful to waste a good gag because you haven't shot enough dead time once the punchline's been delivered. You only need for it to happen twice. We used a small lightweight 16mm camera so that we could keep the movement fluid and natural. It was important to let the camera become secondary to the performance. It was also important for me to capture each gag in one take. To lend a more fly-on-the-wall feel to the series, as if it was captured just as it happened. I learned a lot about being scared. If you're doing something that's never been done before, or that you've never done before, I suppose it's only natural. Butterflies in your stomach equals good. Generally, the process of some-

thing this exciting is disappointing, but MTV was amazing. Once they commissioned it, I was on autopilot with my crew and it was one of the best production experiences I've had to date.'

ON AIR

'I've received such good feedback to the series. Everybody seems to have their favourite. Having an MTV clip on my reel is a good thing. It's an endorsement by those who sponsor creativity, by association. People assume that you take creative risks. I was impressed by the way MTV gave me

such complete creative freedom once they commissioned the idea. If creativity is best defined as one person's truth, doing something for MTV is a good way to explore yours.'

addicted

MTV asia

CHER Campbell

ATTITUDE: 'I'm creative from necessity. I can't express myself very well. My thoughts don't always, or hardly ever, make sense to other people, so I like to dress these thoughts up in pretty little bows; that way, people think they look nice, even if they don't get it.'

LOCATION: Singapore

CLIENTS: Heineken, Nokia, Nabisco, HSBC, Levi's, British Columbia Lottery Corporation, Corby Distilleries

MTV DIRECTOR, ON AIR PROMOTIONS, CREATIVE AND CONTENT: Charmaine Choo

AGENCY: Bates Singapore

CREATIVE TEAM: Cher Campbell, Pam Fraser

DIRECTOR: James Brown

PRODUCTION HOUSE: Stink

CONCEPT

'I was working on a music-related brief for one of our clients. I kept thinking about how me and my best friend liked to translate American top 40 pop songs into French (she's French) and leave the ridiculous sounding translation on each other's voice mail. I then realised that most lyrics were kind of silly in translation. One of my favourites and one that I just couldn't manage to make work is this little gem from Prince. "Animals strike curious poses when they feel the heat; the heat between you and me." We presented the idea almost exactly as it was, with the unnamed client's product figuring prominently in each spot. The client didn't much care for it, so we took it to MTV. They loved it. We made it.'

MAKING IT

'The biggest challenge was budget. We had about 15 talents for the four spots. So a lot of the budget had to go on paying those guys, which didn't leave much for little things, like the film. Fortunately, people were willing to do stuff for nothing or almost nothing because it was for MTV.'

ON AIR

'Doing a campaign for MTV means that people in advertising tend to judge it quite harshly. They think that if it's MTV it's easy to do something good; but that's not the case. It is not easier to have a great idea for MTV than to have a great idea for crackers. The results have been great, the campaign was a finalist at Cannes and it picked up a bunch of other awards as well. We tried to produce a body of work that could safely air across all of the channels that make up MTV Asia. This means taking into account the different cultural and religious mores for each country.'

REBEL WITHOUT A PAUSE

SOPHIE LOVELL

MTV was born with a rebellious, out of the box attitude. It arrived at a time when teenagers were still called teenagers, young people still craved everything and anything that their parents hated, and the generation gap had not yet closed. But now we live in a design-conscious society where supposedly 'everything goes' so what is there left to rebel against? Does MTV still maintain and still need this image?

MTV has come a long way from the simple link and clips formula of the 1980s. The company has changed a lot and so have its objectives. It has become much more complex than just a music channel, it has become a complete entertainment package for young people. In some ways this means that what is on offer is a whole lot richer and more interesting, but it also means that it has become a lot more commercial. MTV needs to work hard if it wants to continue to live up to this rebellious, original and alternative image. It has to continually ask itself how best it can do business according to the rules of the commercial world, while giving viewers a strong alternative, non-conventional message. MTV also needs to ask these questions separately, in each and every regional and genre channel because, it has now reached a stage when the answers are not always necessarily what one might expect.

'We don't have much of a punk attitude in Japan', says Miyako Hattori, former executive producer of On-Air Promos and Creative, MTV Japan, 'but I think that we show an attitude that says we understand young people and can communicate with them.'

MTV in Japan is not so much a rebel as a friend, she explains; 'In a class at school there's always a popular kid who is not goody-goody or dumb, but cool, that's what we'd like to be, smart and cool but in a mainstream way.' She acknowledges that the rebel attitude is part of MTV heritage, it goes with the territory and still needs to be maintained, but adds, 'anti-establishment is not part of our branding'.

For Maurice Hols, channel director, MTV Netherlands, the anti-establishment image of MTV is very much present and maintained at a human level via the VJs and presenters; 'Our presenters have to be rebellious. We have a punk band called Spider Rico and the singer Dennis Weening is a presenter with us. If we want to do something non-conformist, then he's our guy.'

At MTV Russia, rebellious attitude is a creative state of mind. 'We're non-political, active, fast moving and we're flexible', says Ivan Bogdanov, creative director at MTV Russia, 'that always goes with an anti-establishment image. We are trying to push the boundaries of people's perceptions. That's being rebellious, because often people don't want to think.'

Lars Beckung, creative director at MTV Nordic is concerned that being rebellious these days is somewhat self-defeating, 'when the average age at a concert is 35 and Tony Blair says he loves Franz Ferdinand'. For Beckung, traditional alternative routes are no longer viable and the issue of how to stay 'different' is more relevant; 'Our core attributes are to be ground-breaking and unexpected so that people are surprised and sometimes shocked at what they see'.

If you are a big media brand then it is rather hard to stay underground, he says, but MTV Nordic still find space for music that is occasionally not mainstream and for experimental graphics; 'A friend of mine who works for one of the terrestrial channels recently told me: "You are crazy to show black and white arty-farty shit. Aren't you losing viewers left, right and centre?" So I'd say we're not really rebellious but just different.'

MTV UK with its five channels concentrates its non-conformist attitude on the highly interactive MTV2 where it relies on its viewers to keep it edgy. Georgia Cooke, head of UK On-Air: 'MTV2 maintains its kind of edge with the audience through language. The whole identity is built around speaking to the audience and them speaking back.'

Cam Levin, vice president, Creative, MTV Networks International, believes that it is not so much a question of being rebellious as being thought-provoking, 'I think we do that by constantly asking ourselves whether we are asking ourselves enough questions'. Whereas Alejandro Abramovich, director, On-Air

MTV Networks Latin America is an MTV traditionalist and says, 'MTV is expected to break rules, if MTV is not breaking rules then it is not doing its job; otherwise it's just one more channel and not worth watching'.

But MTV has many faces in many lands and in some countries being a rebel is most definitely not cool. 'In Asia', says Charmaine Choo, director, On-Air Promotions, MTV Networks Asia, 'we try to be irreverent, but it's just not the Asian way. Asian culture tells you to respect your elders and your family. We poke gentle fun but it has to be at a level that works for our audience.'

Rebellion is 'not something we go for' says Cyrus Oshidar, senior vice president, Creative and Content, MTV India; 'At the age of 41 I still hide the fact I smoke from my parents. Ours is not a culture of rebellion. We are not trying to be anti-establishment.'

Staying edgy and rebellious is no big deal believes Maurizio Vitale, former vice president, creative director for MTV South, as long as you take care to employ the right kind of people. With the right creative team, being different and having interesting ideas has more to do with instinct than design; There is no big strategy, it comes from the heart, from the stomach. In this sense, MTV is very lucky because it is still living off the memory of a legend. In the 1980s this channel was like nothing else that had come before. It was like an alien. People were watching MTV as if it were Jesus Christ. It was a doctrine, a philosophy, a trend; it was everything. I think that to a certain extent MTV is probably still benefitting from those years.'

Where cultural differences really do come into play is with the question of taste and permissiveness. Some regions have strong moral codes that are either self-enforced or enforced by the state, some are very relaxed but their audiences are jaded by years of sensationalist taboo-breaking, and there are others that are still not sure how far they can go because nobody has really tried yet. The variety of invisible walls can be fascinating. Holland has an incredible amount of freedom says Maurice Hols, but even they have limits; 'Only once we had a

"Viva la Bam" poster that had to be removed because it showed a fat guy sitting in a chair with ropes around him and it didn't look very nice.'

Maurizio Vitale explains the situation in Southern Europe; 'Every market is a different reality', and 'I would say that generally Southern Europe has less problems with showing, say, sexual content. Not in every country though, because this is obviously heavily influenced by the political moment the country is going through. For example, we are going through a very bad political moment in Italy. The country is run by a very conservative government. Very conservative means that you can't show certain things at certain times of the day, content such as homosexuality and sex. We are obliged to put that kind of stuff on quite late at night. We do have a very good moment right now in Spain, however, because it has a left-wing, socialist government, which is progressive and modern and open to different subjects and cultures. For example, if you had a campaign on a social issue, like wearing a condom, with some explicit imagery, it would not be a problem in Spain but it would be in Italy.'

Politics is one issue that is loaded with confrontation wherever you are in the world, even in the UK, says Georgia Cooke; 'We have a highly-developed regulatory body here called Ofcom. In the UK you can't actually transmit an unbalanced political opinion. MTV Germany, for example, took a political anti-war stance during the Iraq War. We can't do that, we can't be seen to be biased. So from that point of view it is sometimes quite difficult to be a youth channel and broadcast something that is actually meaningful to the audience.'

In Latin America religion is an issue. 'You wouldn't want to go against the Catholic Church because it's not worth it', says Alejandro Abramovich, 'we don't mess much with politics either. I would like to, I think we could, it would be risky, it would get us in trouble, but the reason we don't do it is we don't have the resources to fight that fight.'

Ivan Bogdanov on the other hand doesn't believe that confrontation is a particularly valid form of

rebellion at all; 'When you're too confrontational you stop being intelligent. You can still be interesting by gently pushing the envelope.'

In Asia too, says Charmaine Choo, 'we'd avoid being confrontational in the first place. I don't think it works. We're not anti-establishment or anti-family; we're the opposite.'

When it comes to who best fills the 'alternative' niché competition from other brands does not even seem to be an issue for MTV. The Network is the undisputed leader of the pack in the realm of creative youth channels. Or, as Maurice Hols so succinctly puts it; 'We don't compete with them, we own them!'

And for the channels that MTV does not yet own, the brand's image is so strong that most others seem pale in comparison. Georgia Cook again; 'MTV is a really powerful thing. The others are commercially-based channels. They don't do anything for their audiences that isn't about ratings. We've got more creative and editorial flexibility than they have. The only way they can talk to their audience is through music, whereas we respond and have a dialogue with our audience through youth culture.'

But MTV has grown enormously, and at 25-years-old is pretty much over the hill by its own standards. Does it still have the right to even pretend that it can still be confrontational and anti-establishment?

'Yes absolutely', says Cam Levin, 'Although MTV is part of one of the world's largest media companies, it's still relevant locally. It's very autonomous as well. Each channel or region has its own team, its own creative direction, its own business strategy and it's own values. By that token it doesn't feel like a big multinational corporation is imposing on anyone. It's giving local regions the chance to air music videos and everything that surrounds them on their own channel and with their own voice.'

DIRTY SANCHEZ: JOBS FOR THE BOYOS

REGION

MTV UK

ARTIST

SCOTT RAWSTHORNE

ATTITUDE: 'I want to make something totally unexpected and face the challenges that make me feel nervous and excited.'
LOCATION: London, UK
CLIENTS: MTV UK, MTV2, MTV Hits, MTV Base, Flextech TV

CREDITS

MTV HEAD OF CREATIVE: Georgia Cooke
DIRECTOR, WRITER: Scott Rawsthorne
PRODUCER: Bernie Costello
MUSIC: Welsh National Anthem

CONCEPT
'MTV UK commissioned this trailer to launch series two of "Dirty Sanchez". The idea was based around a fictional crash test facility, that has been set up to test the stunts in the show.'

MAKING IT
'It was shot on super 16mm in half a day, using an ARRI camera. Most of the spots were shot at 100 frames per second to capture the explosions. The most difficult thing was the limited time; in an ideal world we should have had a full day to shoot not four hours.'

ON AIR
'The spot was nominated for a Promax award in November 2004 and was generally well received.'

10 años

MTV Latin America

Gabriel Sagel / In Jaus

ATTITUTE: 'To be original, memorable, distinctive and true to the brand's spirit with no generic advertising clichés.'
LOCATION: Buenos Aires, Argentina
CLIENTS: MTV, Space, ISat, Playboy, FTV, MuchMusic, Venus, Retro, Radio Disney, Arcor, Bodegas Bianchi, Diario Olé, Fox Italy

MTV DIRECTOR, ON AIR:
Alejandro Abramovich
PRODUCER: Fernando Lazzari,
MTV Networks Latin America
AGENCY: In Jaus
DIRECTOR: Gabriel Sagel
CREATIVE DIRECTOR: Esteban Pigni
EXECUTIVE PRODUCER: Gabriel Starna
COPYWRITERS: Marcos Calandrelli,
Diego Medvedocky
POST-PRODUCTION: Federico Torres
PRODUCTION COMPANY: In Jaus Films

CONCEPT

G. Sagel: 'The idea evolved from some not very funny gags involving two cleaning ladies to some very funny ideas involving the same characters. We thought about how MTV had changed people's lives in these last 10 years and that their own staff, the cleaners were a good starting point.'

F. Lazzari: 'We gave the guys at In Jaus in Buenos Aires a very precise brief and they quickly came up with this idea that we instantly loved; it was very simple, irreverent and straightforward. I liked the idea of the cleaning ladies' point of view on different MTV themes such as Pop versus Rock or the Madonna-Britney kiss. It seemed a very smart and appropriate way to talk about our brand. One of the spots got a Bronze Lion in Cannes, which is remarkable considering the ultra-low budget they had to work with.'

MAKING IT

G. Sagel: 'The main challenge was the budget. All three spots were shot on Sony High Definition cameras in one day.'

F. Lazzari: 'In Jaus were incredibly fast at conceptualising and producing this piece. They used high definition cameras, which worked very well. I think the main challenge here was the casting of the ladies, which was really fantastic. They had to be not just great actresses, but also they had to fake a neutral accent and be willing to kiss each other in front of the camera. Of course, the art direction, wardrobe and camera work were key in the success of the project.'

ON AIR

G. Sagel: 'We learned that our budget was small, the actresses were great and that working for MTV is a lot of fun.'

F. Lazzari: 'This campaign aired for the first time during the VMA Latin America 2003, which is a moment of peak ratings at our channel. It created a lot of buzz, both within the industry and among our audiences. Fortunately, we didn't have any standard issues and the campaign aired everywhere.'

BRAD & ERIC USED CAR UNIVERSE

MTV BENELUX

JOHN DOE AMSTERDAM

ATTITUDE: 'John Doe's philosophy is no bullshit just good work. Work makes work.'
LOCATION: Amsterdam, the Netherlands
CLIENTS: MTV, Bacardi, Lada, Tetra Pak, Johan magazine, City Council Rotterdam, Martini

MTV CREATIVE DIRECTOR: Danny Smit
CONCEPT: John Doe, Amsterdam
CREATIVE, COPY: Hein Mevissen, Rob Doubal, Attila Kiraly, Diederiekje Bok
PRODUCTION: Denise Stork, Levi Munch
DIRECTOR: Hein Mevissen
DOP: Bianca van Riemsdijk
PRODUCER: Francine vand er Lee, John Doe
SOUND: Studio de Keuken / Geert van Galen
MUSIC: R Crumb and The Cheap Suit Serenaders / Shopping Mall

CONCEPT

'The concept is based on a true story and is about Brad and Eric, two brothers who own a scrap yard, "Brad and Eric's Used Car Universe", and spend their time doing a lot of nonsense. Brad in particular has his own special theories about the world. Every new MTV commercial that John Doe Amsterdam makes is meant to inspire the creative target group of MTV. For this particular concept John Doe made 12 commercials about Brad and Eric's Used Car Universe. Brad and Eric are very successful, they have their own fan club and have been asked to do a TV show on MTV; the "Brad and Eric Show".'

MAKING IT

'The really difficult part about making the clip were Brad and Eric's conversations. We had a lot of scripts for them and in the end had to choose the best. The films were shot in the suburbs of New Jersey. We did the post-production in Amsterdam.'

ON AIR

'We never expected Brad and Eric to be that much of a success. Surprisingly a lot of people got Brad's absurd jokes and the dry humour of his theories. Every day we get a lot of questions about Brad and Eric. Many compliments came from MTV and other regions such as MTV Nordic, MTV Spain and MTV New Zealand who wanted to show these films as well. MTV Benelux is different from other clients in that they trust John Doe and love to be surprised by our work. At the end of every month we present MTV with a new film. Our next project will be made on Tonger Island, close to New Zealand. MTV has not given us a script or a concept; they will just wait for our surprise.'

Love Weekend

MTV Italy

Vera Braghiroli

ATTITUDE: 'To make a message understandable for the target and then tailor it with an attitude suitable to the occasion'.
LOCATION: Milan, Italy
CLIENTS: MTV Italy, Filmaster Clip, Diesel Italia

DIRECTOR: Vera Braghiroli
GRAPHIC DESIGNER: Lorenzo Banal
DOP: Eugenio Galli
PRODUCTION COMPANY: MADE srl
STYLING: Vera Braghiroli
POST-PRODUCTION: 3D-Vision
EDITING VIDEO: Vera Braghiroli
EDITING AUDIO: Mach2
MUSIC: Livio Magnini, Pass the Hatchet

CONCEPT

'Initially, there was no intention to promote these two special days of video clip selections inspired by St Valentine. Then we had the idea of making it a brand communication opportunity by playing down the romantic cliché and turning it upside down in an ironic way. We based it on the fake promotion of a couple of videotapes containing a collection of extremely sentimental and naive video clips, for "slumped" couples eager to warm up their relationships; ready-made love as an unexpected aphrodisiac.'

MAKING IT

'Because the budget was only 3,500 euros, we had just one day shooting in Mini DV with a small crew, one day for editing and one for compositing. It was done in-house with the help of our graphic designer. To avoid the risk of lapsing into viagra-style vulgarity, we needed an improbable couple of characters, to give the promo a touch of sur-realism. The main problem was finding perfectly suited interpreters. The location hunting wasn't easy either, because we couldn't afford to furnish a studio, we had to look for real interiors. The one we ended up using is a flat belonging to a friends grandfather.'

ON AIR

'The promo turned out to be entertaining and quite convincing, since MTV received some phone calls from viewers asking where they could buy these videotapes. It took a press release to clarify possible misunderstandings, which gave an extra plug to our channel programming.'

SHEEP

MTV IRELAND, MTV UK

NICK RYAN / IMAGE NOW FILMS

ATTITUDE: 'Telling good stories well.'
LOCATION: Dublin, Ireland
CLIENTS: MTV, Adobe, Avonmore Cream, Boru Vodka, Ford, Eagle Star

MTV HEAD OF CREATIVE: Georgia Cooke
DIRECTOR: Nick Ryan
PRODUCER: Seamus Byrne
ART DIRECTOR: Dylan Davies
COPYWRITER: Emmett Wright
DOP: James Mather
MUSIC: The Chalets
CAST: Bernd Deegan

CONCEPT

'MTV asked us to create some graphics to fill a potential gap in advertising schedules during the start-up phase of MTV Ireland. I felt there was an opportunity to create something a bit more interesting. How did the idea evolve? I wanted a humorous take on a situation; to create a character and show what he does for a living. I worked with a writer, Emmet Wright, from an agency in Dublin, and outlined an approach. He came back with a few different stories and I felt the best was the one about an ex-stylist to the stars who has decided to take his work in a new direction.'

MAKING IT

'Casting the right stylist was the first challenge, and Bern Deegan had the right charisma to carry it off. Casting the sheep was interesting. They are remarkably calm and really took to Bern; very stylish sheep. The main challenge was in training the sheep to sit in the chairs. Sheep are great actors. We shot for one a day using a Panasonic AG DVX100A Camera and film lighting. Post-production was about a week. It was edited in Discreet Logic Edit, plus some matte painting in Photoshop with 3D in Softimage XSI and compositing with After Effects.'

ON AIR

'MTV loved it, and so did the audience. It was meant to run for six weeks but ended up on air for over a year due to the positive feedback.'

TITLE

MTV VIDEO MUSIC AWARDS
JAPAN 2003

REGION

MTV JAPAN

ARTIST

ISAO NISHIGORI

LOCATION: Tokyo, Japan
CLIENTS: Matsushita Electric Industrial
Co Ltd, SSL Health Care Japan Ltd, River
Japan, MTV Japan Inc

CREDITS

MTV EXECUTIVE PRODUCER ON AIR
PROMOS AND CREATIVE: Miyako Hattori
DIRECTOR: Isao Nishigori
OFFICE: PICS Co, Ltd
MUSIC: Kiyoshi Hazemoto

CONCEPT

'Since the concept for this event was, waves of music, I thought it will be interesting to adapt hair waves to the patterns of sound waves.'

MAKING IT

'The main difficulty was including the tremendous number of award titles and their accompanying ideas in the clip. I shot with an HD camera and then used Maya for the fluid movements. During shooting, there was nothing on top of the head so I had to imagine what the final picture would look like as we went along, which was not easy. However challenging, this difficult task was nevertheless very exciting and I enjoyed it very much.'

ON AIR

'The feedback we received after the clip had been on air wasn't bad at all. With this clip I realised again how hard it is to use an optically-composed technique when making a film.'

TITLE

MUSIC AND MORE

REGION

MTV JAPAN

ARTIST

IZMO JUKI,
HIROSHI KIZU

ATTITUDE: 'Creativity is always what
you believe.' (I. Juki)
LOCATION: Tokyo, Japan
CLIENTS: MTV Japan, Microsoft XBOX,
Capcom, Nexon Japan, Kirin Brewery, Aoi
Advertising Promotion,

CREDITS

MTV EXECUTIVE PRODUCER ON AIR
PROMOS AND CREATIVE: Miyako Hattori
DIRECTOR: Hiroshi Kizu
PRODUCTION DESIGN, CHARACTER
DESIGN: Junji Okubo and Izmo Juki
CGI: SPICE Inc
VISUAL EFFECT SUPERVISOR:
Joji Hayashi / SPICE Inc
MUSIC: Jaermulk Manhattan
VOICE PERFORMANCE:
Maaya Sakamoto / Victor Entertainment Inc

CONCEPT

I. Juki: 'I was invited to participate in this project by the MTV director Hiroshi Kizu in early 2004, and became involved from the initial planning stages. The idea was to present MTV as media focused; not only delivering music but also providing something more, something extra. We had the idea of creating an imaginary robot that constructs the beat by cutting up everyday sounds as samples. The message is that these sounds and MTV are closely connected. Also, it represents the visual stimulation of something as it is transformed.'

MAKING IT

I. Juki: 'During production, Hiroshi Kizu started working on the storyboard and I designed the robot, the main character, as well as the BGM. Once I had finished designing my character, the shooting started. About a week later we began with the post-production. Then, we sent the robot designs, which also included 3D modelling data, and the background material to a computer generating production company to do the CGI part. It took about a month and a half to complete the production. Although I've done lots of character designs for games, comics and composite pictures before, this was my first experience with live-action film; so it was a big challenge for me. The production schedule was also extremely tight, so I carefully designed in detail to avoid any problems at the post-production stage. When it comes to this kind of character design, being visually convincing is an important feature. When making something imaginary that does not exist, you need to trick the audience. Since the reproduction of reality is usually emphasised by DV shooting, I worked particularly hard on this part. At the CGI composition stage, the matching technique was done with HD lighting and it really helped the production.'

ON AIR

I. Juki: 'I grew up watching MTV when I was a teenager, so I was very happy to work on its image spot; but then I didn't get any feedback afterwards because people in Japan prefer robots with a more personalised character, it was probably not interesting to them. This movie clip was only shown in Japan, but when I put it on my website, I got an offer from a foreign publisher to feature my work and they have invited me to participate in making a movie.'

CHASING HORSES

MTV KOREA

ALICE EXP

ATTITUDE: 'We are not making UFOs or aliens, which do not exist in the world, we like sharing something that exists; transforming things or mixing them with our philosophy.'

LOCATION: Seoul, Korea

CLIENTS: MTV Korea, Ludens Films, EGG Films, Hanty, Mutsallim MaDang

MTV DIRECTOR, ON AIR PROMOS AND CREATIVE SERVICES: Es Lim
DIRECTORS: Jo Se-Heon, Jo Seong-Yoon
EXECUTIVE PRODUCER: Lim Eung-Seok
2D AND 3D ANIMATION: Jo Seong-Yoon
EDITED BY: Jo Se-Heon
MUSIC: Jun-Seop
SOUND DESIGN: Jo Se-Heon

CONCEPT

'In Spring 2004, Alice Exp was asked to direct a couple of station idents for the MTV Korea on-air promotions team. We had already directed a station ident, called the Enerpia for MTV Korea in 2001, which was when Alice Exp was established, and MTV Korea was preparing the launch of their 24-hour channel. The Enerpia concept came from a traditional Korean painting, "Ship Jang Seng", and received a good response from local and international companies. As a result, the Enerpia motivated the Chasing Horses project. Chasing Horses was inspired by some famous Korean earthenware treasures called the "Horse-Riding Warriors". We found these sculptures in a museum and felt that we needed to give them real lives and make them run really fast. Also we were still full of the mysterious energy from the endless grasslands and deserts of the Gobi desert, which we travelled through three years ago. This was how the idea for Chasing Horses came about; we wanted to make "Horse-Riding Warriors" run through the Gobi desert. We wanted to share this feeling with other people.'

MAKING IT

'During the production process, the main aim was to make the warriors fast and alive. First, the running action was created with the 3D-rendered lower part of the M in MTV. Then, it was put together with the upper part of the M using Adobe After Effects and then animated to make it look more real and alive. Since we wanted to make a thousand of these MTV M's run from a side-view angle, we made three parts, a near view, middle view and a distant view. Each aspect of colour, tone, speed and focus was handled separately. Also, we spent a lot of time mixing 2D with 3D because we didn't want to lose the dimension of the 3D objects and the texture of

the 2D objects in the mixing sequence. Another problem was to match up the music with sound effects. It was extremely difficult to match up and synch fast beats, explosion effects and the sound of horses' hooves. The tools we used were; Mac G4 1.25 dual, Mac G4 800, 2.5 PC, After Effects, Light Wave, Photoshop, Illustrator, Apple Soundtrack and Pro Tools.'

ON AIR

'When the clip was broadcast we received a lot of positive reactions from viewers who said that it re-interpreted Korean tradition in a new modern style. The Chasing Horses project is one of the best accomplishments of Alice Exp.'

TITLE

Tamoo

REGION

MTV Korea

ARTIST

Song Min-Wook

ATTITUDE: 'I'm driven by the urge to create something that doesn't exist in the world.'
LOCATION: Seoul, Korea
CLIENTS: MTV Korea, KBS, SBS

CREDITS

MTV DIRECTOR, ON AIR PROMOS AND CREATIVE SERVICES: Es Lim
EXECUTIVE PRODUCER: Lim Eung-Seok
DIRECTOR: Song Min-Wook
ANIMATOR: Kwak Ho-Hyung
DESIGNER: Ko Seung-Eun
EDITOR: Kwak Ho-Hyung, Song Min-Wook
SOUND: Park Issac, Seo Jae-Min

CONCEPT

'The original creatures were produced by VirusHead. Using their characters, I presented them in a cute and funny manner with the intention of developing them further into a television series. Tamoo is a story about nine humanised-animals who live in a small town and each one of them has an exotic personality. The MTV Tamoo project was created in response to a direct request from MTV Korea and started when the original book was published. Since it was a kind of promotional vehicle for the book, I put particular emphasis on the characters and made warmer images of them with colourful artwork that felt more like MTV's style.'

MAKING IT

'Like with our other clip Marx Clay, we tried to create a new style of artwork, with very little budget and just a few members of staff. We worked on this project for about a month but if we consider the development of the entire idea, then it took much longer. What really helped to finalise the project was the trust between members of staff. We used Photoshop, Illustrator, Flash MX, After Effects and Painter.'

ON AIR

'Having MTV as a client is a great attraction. There is a kind of confidence in tone and quality that can be interpreted from the name of MTV. The most important aspect of working with MTV is that it considers the personality and thoughts of the artist, unlike many clients. Also, MTV tries to seek out the MTV style within the various artist's personalities, which makes it very enjoyable to work with MTV.'

MARX CLAY

MTV KOREA

SONG MIN-WOOK

ATTITUDE: 'I'm driven by the urge to create something that doesn't exist in the world.'
LOCATION: Seoul, Korea
CLIENTS: MTV Korea, KBS, SBS

MTV DIRECTOR, ON AIR PROMOS AND CREATIVE SERVICES: Es Lim
EXECUTIVE PRODUCER: Lim Eung-Seok
DIRECTOR: Song Min-Wook
ANIMATOR: Kwak Ho-Hyung
DESIGNER: Ko Seung-Eun
EDITOR: Kwak Ho-Hyung, Song Min-Wook
SOUND: Song Byung-Jeun

CONCEPT

'The character Marx Clay is made of clay and his face can be transformed into any shape. Marx Clay works in a bakery where one day he finds out about his boss's evil plan to put some bad drugs in the bread in order to conquer the whole world. Marx Clay tries to stop him but gets thrown into the drugs barrel instead. The effect of the drugs on him means that Marx acquires the ability to transform his face into any shape. The boss builds up military forces in the underground city and tries to spread his power all around the globe. But Marx, the hero, stands up to the power of darkness. After a brainstorming session, we generated some good ideas and chose the one we thought could easily be developed into a TV series since that was what the clip was originally created for. Because the clip is part of a longer story, it was difficult to shorten it. We discussed it with MTV Korea who commissioned the clip and decided to make it into a fast-paced movie EPK or TVC.'

MAKING IT

'We tried to create a new style of artwork and we also attempted to achieve high quality on a low budget. The latter was the hardest part of the whole production process. I decided to leave out the stage of firstly drawing on paper and scanning that. Instead, the animator and director drew pictures directly onto the computer screen. During this project we definitely learned the art of cutting costs. Production took about a month but in fact the idea was in development for much longer. We used Photoshop, Illustrator, Flash MX, After Effects and Painter. The most important issue during the production process was to bring my thoughts together with the style of MTV. We had a lot of discussions with MTV about timing, colour and especially the use of the MTV logo.'

ON AIR

'Needless to say, the influence of the MTV brand is extremely powerful everywhere in the world. The main difference between MTV and other clients is that MTV considers the personalities and thoughts of the artist. The effect of having the clip on air is that now Warner Brothers have shown an interest in it.'

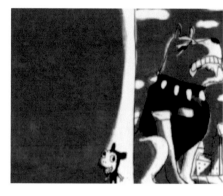

PRO-SOCIAL:
TEACHING
NOT PREACHING

anne-celine jaeger

Up to a billion people have access to MTV in all four corners of the globe. It has the ears and eyes of the young and impressionable, the streetwise and savvy, the inexperienced and vulnerable, the most sexually active and adventurous sections of society. How much of a duty does MTV have to use its influence to educate and inform by sacrificing valuable airspace to social issues?

Whether shooting an Indian VJ out of a cheap-looking cannon with the slogan 'Whatever risks you take in life, don't take risks in love' so as to promote safe sex, or setting up an 'Express yourself' booth at a music festival, to encourage teenagers to speak out about issues, MTV is always coming up with strategies to promote social awareness. Indeed, in most regions, pro-social activity has become such an integral part of programming that it is now very much a part of the worldwide brand.

'We have a social responsibility', says Cam Levin, vice president, Creative, MTV Networks International. *'Because we are working with an extremely impressionable audience, we have a duty to be pro-social as well as entertaining. Our aim is to provoke thoughts and raise awareness around issues that young people are thinking about without ever being preachy.'*

Now that MTV has 46 channels around the world, with a potential viewing audience of more than one billion people, it goes without saying that the approach to pro-social issues will not always be homogenous. Just as the look and feel of each MTV channel varies considerably from region to region, so too do the issues that they may want to tackle, the ways in which they choose to do so and the budgets available.

When it comes to addressing the audience, India for example is confronted by a whole different set of challenges than of the European territories. Cyrus Oshidar, senior vice president, Creative and Content, MTV India says; *'In India we're completely immune to suffering. Millions may die in an earthquake overnight. We're used to being in a state of shock.'*

Consequently, fresh methods of capturing the audience are a necessity. According to Oshidar, hu-

mour is the best way to get through to his viewers. *'It's difficult to pick an issue and be serious about it. In order for any message to stay in young people's heads these days, we need to use a healthy dose of humour. If we scared the shit out of our young viewers, they'd never listen.'* Hence the clip of the VJ being catapulted out of a cheap-looking cannon...

MTV Russia is fighting a similar battle, but rather than dealing with compassion fatigue, they are faced with the aftermath of the Perestroika, which brought with it an apathy towards any type of social activity. Ivan Bogdanov, creative director at MTV Russia says; *'During the Perestroika, every aspect of cultural life was social. There were so many social messages going on that everybody got tired of it.'* MTV Russia's aim now is to develop a new language that, as Bogdanov says, *'won't alienate all those people'.*

Injecting a pro-social project with a local flavour and voice is also particularly pertinent in Latin America. According to Alejandro Abramovich, director of On-Air MTV Networks Latin America, what works in Argentina would never work in Mexico and vice versa. He says, *'Whereas Mexico adores all things that come from outside their country, the Argentines are proud of their culture and heritage.'*

Hence, MTV Latin America came to the conclusion early on that they had to act absolutely locally. Abramovich says; *'If we want to send out an HIV awareness message to the Argentines, it has to be completely relevant to them. If you put all your efforts and budget into something that is so international that it ends up being neutral, it's not going to work in Argentina.'* This is why the Argentine promo for the Staying Alive campaign is completely home-grown and features a famous Argentinian actor, Fernando Pena, who also wrote the script.

At the other end of the spectrum, there are regions such as MTV Nordic who have to struggle at times to even find local issues. *'As a region we're really blessed,'* says creative director Lars Beckung who looks after the Finnish, Swedish, Norwegian and Danish channels. Nevertheless, MTV Nordic is just as committed to raising awareness about global issues such as HIV or human trafficking as other regions, but the need to get the tone of the spots just right is crucial says Beckung; *'So many messages are beamed out to young people these days that it's easy to get it slightly wrong. And if you get it wrong, you alienate more people. It's difficult to make something that isn't too dark but still gets the message across that it's a big problem. In general, we approach pro-social spots just like everything else. We try to be different. If all HIV campaigns are about condoms, then we'll do something else.'*

MTV Nordic's 'Clean Conscience' areas at the recent Roskilde Festival in Denmark were a good example of tackling social issues from surprising perspectives. These areas contained washing machines where people could wash their clothes together, as well as viewing areas where films about human trafficking were being shown. On a more global level, the 'Save the Humans' ident, that originated in the USA as part of the 'Staying Alive' campaign, works equally well locally as for the rest of the world. 'Save the Humans' is an animation clip that portrays a group of animals sitting around a G8 table discussing how humans need to be helped. *'We just twisted the concept around to make you think about it differently'*, says Beckung.

Enlightened Scandinavians aside, for many countries MTV is, still to this day, the first and only media outlet to highlight sensitive issues such as safe sex. When MTV India launched in 1996, they were the first channel in the sub-continent to use mass communication as a means of stressing the magnitude of the HIV epidemic in their market. Similarly MTV Japan, even now, is one of the few Japanese media outlets to broach the subject of HIV awareness. Miyako Hattori, former executive producer of On Air Promos and Creative, MTV Japan says, *'Lots of kids in Japan think HIV is not part of their world, and it doesn't help that terrestrial TV here is very veiled. Most channels don't talk about condoms; but we do.'* One way in which MTV Japan tackled the issue was to run a spot of a VJ going for an HIV test. Hattori says; *'It was a very honest approach and it seemed to be pretty effective.'*

However, due to local religious and/or political influences, not every country where MTV is broadcast is at liberty to be so outspoken on air. MTV Singapore, for example, which also gets broadcast in Malaysia and Indonesia, still can't be seen to be promoting promiscuity or sex before marriage. Charmaine Choo, Director, On-Air Promotions, MTV Networks Asia says; *'Our HIV awareness campaigns, focus more on abstinence than promiscuity. We did a live action spot last year that showed young teenagers rehearsing how to turn someone down.'*

Although having a visual aesthetic is always a vital component of each pro-social campaign, such as the animated G8 animals or the raw confessions of Asian youths, it is not the ultimate objective. Cam Levin emphasises that there is no point in having an exceptional looking spot if the concept behind it doesn't work; *'If you don't have a good idea, it doesn't matter how well you dress it up; it will just pass over people's heads as something seductive for 30 seconds and then be forgotten. If you have a strong idea that is badly made, it can leave more of an impression than something that is extremely well made but with no idea behind it at all.'*

In many ways, Levin's comments are an encouragement because one of the main challenges faced by all regions when producing a pro-social campaign, is the budgetary restriction. More often than not, funds for generating a spot must either be derived from each channel's on-air budget or, if they are lucky, from financial partners such as charities or NGOs. At MTV India doing things on the cheap – like the home-made cannon – is born out of necessity but it does work very well when it comes to getting the message across.

According to Oshidar, the channel is designed to be imperfect, because that's what India is; *'Part of the joy of being at MTV is finding ways around budgetary problems; that's when the good stuff happens. Often we'll even squeeze in a live action pro-social shoot starring a VJ between takes for another show. We use whatever tools we have.'*

Thankfully, MTV is a channel that welcomes blunders; or, as Ivan Bogdanov of MTV Russia puts it; *'It's a huge laboratory for people to try things out. You can make mistakes, but they are made honestly, so it doesn't matter.'*

Aside from broadcasting spots, MTV also encourages social awareness by reacting to global and local catastrophes. Following the aftermath of the Asian tsunami in February 2005, for example, MTV held a global fundraising concert in Bangkok called MTV Asia Aid. Similarly, after the Nigata earthquake in Japan in October 2004, MTV Japan produced endorsements by local artists and asked the audience for donations. These are only a couple of examples, but they are an indication of the channels' commitment to prodding the public conscience.

Ethical initiatives have become a trademark of the brand and are now starting to move beyond the on-air realm into real life; and there is no dearth of ideas either. Former vice president, creative director MTV South, Maurizio Vitale would like to see the channel extend event sponsorship from commercial clients to NGOs; *'We should definitely have more initiatives: we do parties for commercial clients so we should do parties for non-profit organisations as well.'*

In Holland, channel director Maurice Hols is keen to make social awareness an integral part of in-house interaction; *'One of our new objectives for next year is to bring social awareness into the company by helping colleagues for example. I think it's important to not only create this feeling on the channel but also within your team.'*

The quest for raising awareness is clearly a worthy and admirable aim and MTV's possession of the ears and eyes of a huge section of the globe's youth carries with it an enormous responsibility. Cam Levin again; *'We are working with an audience who are extremely impressionable and we are putting opinions in place about the world.'*

Nevertheless there is a palpable desire to use this responsibility to do good. *'As a channel, we would like to be doing so much more. We have the ability to really impact lives,'* says India's Cyrus Oshidar. These are sentiments shared by many of MTV's managers and directors.

What is fascinating is how effectively the system manages to regulate which pro-social messages are actually chosen to be supported on air. Certainly there are broadcast regulations to be observed in particular countries, that limit not only what can be said but how it can be said as well. But there seems to be a general MTV consensus that says, 'yes' to social issues, 'no' if there is political content, and above all the golden rule is, 'no preaching'. MTV must never be seen to be playing teacher or parent. Cyrus Oshidar again; *'It's not that we want to tell our audience what to think. We'd just like to inspire them to think so they can formulate their own opinions.'*

It does not appear to be a list of written rules or strict policy guidelines that polices the extent of MTV's social conscience and activities, but an inherent aversion to actively dictating to its audience, or in the words of Brent Hansen, President of Creative & Editor in Chief, MTV Networks International; *'We might bring up the pro's and con's, but we would try not to get in a situation where we act in loco parentis.'*

PACTO 02, ESTATUTO DA CRIANÇA E DO ADOLESCENTE

MTV BRAZIL

LUCIANA NUNES VIEIRA

ATTITUDE: 'My inspiration? The world around me; anything can be an inspiration.'
LOCATION: São Paulo, Brazil
CLIENTS: MTV Brazil, Motorola, Nike, Kibon, Vivo

MTV PROMO MANAGER: Rodrigo Pimenta
DIRECTOR: Luciana Nuners Vieira
ART DIRECTOR: Luciana Nuners Vieira, Jimmy Leroy
PRODUCER: Luciana Nuners Vieira, Tito Livio
CREATIVE WRITER: Mauro Dahmer

CONCEPT

'Pacto is a series of promos primarily intended to raise people's consciousness. Pacto 02 is about the rights of children and adolescents. It was the first stage of a campaign; afterwards we made a mini documentary on the subject.'

MAKING IT

'It took a month to make the whole campaign. I used a Mini Digital Video camera and decided to make the entire clip with shadows. I went to a park where children were playing with a Mini DV camera and filmed them. In fact, it was a very simple process, from which I learned to do things with simplicity. The documentary was the main challenge of the entire project.'

ON AIR

'I hope the campaign made people think about the rights of children and adolescents. Although this particular clip had no direct impact on my work, having an MTV clip in my portfolio means a lot to me.'

VOTE FOR SOMETHING CAMPAIGN

MTV US

TED PAULY, ERIC ECKELMANN, PAUL EWEN

ATTITUDE: 'Everybody's creative, it's just a question of how much you obsess over ideas.' (T. Pauly)
LOCATION: New York, USA
CLIENTS: MTV

MTV SVP ON AIR DESIGN AND OFF AIR: Jeffrey Keyton
MTV SVP ON AIR PROMOS: Kevin Mackall
DIRECTED AND WRITTEN BY: Eric Eckelman, Paul Ewen, Ted Pauly

CONCEPT

T. Pauly: 'These spots were made to encourage our viewers to vote in the 2004 elections. The creative idea grew out of strategic considerations; how could we make voting public service announcements that kids wouldn't tune out right away? We tried to use a varied approach; graphics, stock footage and original footage shot in different styles, so that there was no expected format. This way the spots could sneak up on the viewers. We avoided telegraphing our message at the outset and saved it for a kind of abrupt ending. We wanted the taglines to be simple, and potentially upsetting at first. So, one spot cut directly to the tag "Vote for God" before cycling through a variety of "Vote for" slogans that got at the issue of religion in public schools from all sides. The same with "Vote for SUVs", which then cycled through "Vote for Gas", "Vote for Liberty", "Vote for Hybrids", "Vote for Safety", "Vote for Pollution", etc. Each spot ends on "Vote for Something". The idea here was that young people might be persuaded to think about how simple things in their lives such as driving, going to school, listening to music and shopping might be affected by, or have an effect on, politics.'

MAKING IT

T. Pauly: 'The main challenge was wanting to make spots that push buttons and get people thinking while not being allowed to advocate a particular position. The solution was to try to advocate from an MTV perspective; to be provocative and discuss things in a way that might make people uncomfortable, but to be an equal-opportunity provocateur. What we learned from the young voter turnout in the election is that it's pretty hard to measure success; numbers can be stretched to

support any position. It's difficult to impact voter participation, particularly without the leeway to be partisan.'

ON AIR

T. Pauly: 'These spots were done strictly for MTV USA, obviously. I think the experience influenced all of us to try and do more work with social conscience. There were some small restrictions about content, in the interest of trying to keep the spots balanced, but I think we walked the tightrope as well as could be expected.'

HOUSE ARREST

REGION

MTV EUROPE

ARTIST

STRAWBERRYFROG

ATTITUDE: 'Strawberryfrog's mission is to do a more creative, faster and more efficient job than the huge corporate dinosaurs out there, its a pretty good one I think.'
LOCATION: Amsterdam, the Netherlands; New York, USA
CLIENTS: Mitsubishi, Asics, Heineken, Sony Ericsson, Gas Jeans, Coke Light, Old Navy, Ikea, CGEY, Boomer Coalition

CREDITS

CREATIVE DIRECTOR: Dylan Ingham
DIRECTORS: Joe and Ben Dempsy, Rose Hackney Barbour
SCRIPT: Andy Howarth, Martina Langer

CONCEPT

'Strawberryfrog and MTV are an interesting mix. We have similar aims; to bring contemporary creative ideas to a broad market. In this case we wanted to get across a simple, direct point of view, a view shared by the majority and get them to act. MTV champions a cause every year and Aung San Suu Kyi was, and is, in a very special situation, which they wanted to help raise awareness about. We were happy to work alongside them to do this. Strawberryfrog is made up of 25 different cultures between 50 people in our Amsterdam office. Our global spirit is very open and aware of the need to be free and have freedom of speech. The point was to get the fact across that this leader of free speech was under house arrest for nothing more than saying what she believed in. This is wrong; do something about it @ MTV.com.'

MAKING IT

'The script was written by two talented creatives, Andy Howarth and Martina Langer. It was very simple, and we felt the similarity between a teenager's bedroom and a prison cell so we morphed a kid's room into a cell over a time period of one minute or so; it was quite effective. The directors used a layering technique, which meant that we had to shoot the same scene 12 times using a motion control camera. Each time we took something else away from the bedroom and added a little more of the cell.'

ON AIR

'The results were good in some ways; many people went to the site to sign the petition, which led to the imprisonment of Aung San Suu Kyi being revoked, but she decided to stay until all her friends and colleagues were given the same freedom, which is very brave.'

TITLE

TOLERANCE
IMAGE SPOT

REGION

MTV EMERGING MARKETS

ARTIST

CAM LEVIN

ATTITUDE: 'Everyone and anyone has the potential to have good ideas. What is interesting and a real challenge is to bring life to those ideas and have some fun doing it.'
LOCATION: London, UK

CREDITS

MTV HEAD OF PROGRAMMING AND
PRODUCTION: Tanja Flintoff
DIRECTOR: Cam Levin
COMPOSER: Mads Arp
DOP: Alex Surkala
MUSIC: Mads Arp

CONCEPT

'We had a brief to create pro-social messages around the subject of tolerance. This came in the wake of 9/11. Without being too patronising we wanted to promote tolerance as a value that people should be thinking about, hopefully making people ask themselves if they were tolerant and respectful enough of those people and things that were different to themselves. Mads Arps came up with the idea of combining different musical genres into a harmonious soundtrack for the campaign spot, partly because he's a music producer but also because MTV is a music channel and we wanted to represent this. Music is what MTV is about and music is a great leveller and can hopefully communicate the idea of tolerance to a lot of people without having to use worthy language.'

MAKING IT

'The main challenge was creating eight different locations and set designs with eight different actors in one shot and on a budget for one spot.'

ON AIR

'I work at MTV and have only ever directed this project. I enjoyed it immensely, but will probably leave it to other more talented directors in the future.'

made

MTV US

STILETTO NYC

ATTITUDE: 'Trying to surprise ourselves.'
LOCATION: New York, USA
CLIENTS: MTV, Nike, VH1, Res magazine,
VIVA Fernsehen, As Four

MTV SVP ON AIR DESIGN AND OFF AIR:
Jeffrey Keyton
MTV SVP ON AIR PROMOS: Kevin Mackall
CONCEPT, DESIGN: Stiletto
DOP: Tobin Yelland
MUSIC COMPOSER: Malcolm Francis,
Popular Beat Combo

CONCEPT

'Made is a documentary-style programme where MTV helps teens to realise a personal goal. We wanted the intro to be off-beat, with a mix of kids who had their own kind of charm, so the group is kind of awkward and not overly stylised. We recorded real kids talking about their dreams and aspirations. Then we cut them all together to make a verbal collage.'

MAKING IT

'The biggest challenge in this piece was working with non-actors. We wanted kids who were not polished, so that they be as believable. We tried to get them to talk candidly about their goals and aspirations.'

HIGH SCHOOL STORIES

MTV US

STILETTO NYC

ATTITUDE: 'Trying to surprise ourselves.'
LOCATION: New York, USA
CLIENTS: MTV, Nike, VH1, Res magazine,
VIVA Fernsehen, As Four

MTV SVP ON AIR DESIGN AND OFF AIR:
Jeffrey Keyton
MTV SVP ON AIR PROMOS: Kevin Mackall
CONCEPT, DESIGN: stiletto
DOP: Tobin Yelland
MUSIC: Trevor Sias

CONCEPT

'High School Stories is an investigative look at real life scandals, pranks and controversies that happen in high school. We shot the opening on 16mm at a New Jersey high school. We wanted to catch the specific school environment and ambience. We intentionally filmed the school when no one was around and let the voice-overs create the feeling of people being there.'

MAKING IT

'We shot the whole piece in one day. We were lucky to have a great crew that worked really quickly. We shot on 16mm, which we like a lot. The funny thing was being back in a high school for a day.'

TITLE

STaYING aLIVe
CHINa CaMPaIGN:
NINJa, THe eNDURING MaSTeR

REGION

MTV CHINA, WORLDWIDE

ARTIST

KUOYU aNDReW LO

ATTITUDE: 'When one finds a way of doing
things differently, then I consider that to
be creative. I try to do different things each
time I work. It's actually not easy; especially
in a market like China.'
LOCATION: Beijing, Taipei, London
CLIENTS: MTV Networks International,
MTV Asia Networks, MTV China, MTV
Taiwan, Channel [V] Taiwan, Music Labels

CREDITS

MTV SUPERVISING PRODUCER,
HEAD OF ON AIR PROMOS: Andrew Lo
DIRECTOR: Kuoyu Andrew Lo
PRODUCTION: Red Films, Beijing
ANIMATION: Zhao Bin
MUSIC: The Cranes

CONCEPT

'My team and I made this when I was with MTV
China. I was asked to direct an AIDS awareness PSA
that specifically targeted Chinese youth. It was to
be the first AIDS campaign in China that directly
addressed young people, since China was rather
closed to AIDS issues at the time. The brief and
the money all came from MTV Staying Alive. I was
asked to come up with something that was fun,
in the style of MTV, and that would work in China
where censorship is harsh, so it could be aired to
our audience of 78 million. We were lucky enough
to have some senior creatives from the networks
attend one of our brainstorming sessions; one
senior vice president suggested it would be fun to
have a ninja or kung fu fighter in the spot to make
it a bit oriental. So Ninja was born. Since Ninja in
Chinese literally means "enduring warrior", it fits
with the subjects of using condoms and abstain-
ing from sex.'

MAKING IT

'Time was the biggest challenge. We did everything,
film production with motion graphics, within
three weeks.'

ON AIR

'Ninja turned out to be an award winner, both internationally and in China, so everyone was happy.
When we were still in creative development, there
were people saying the idea wouldn't work because
it was too sexual or because the main character is
a Japanese ninja. In China, censorship can affect
anything; and it gets into creative people's heads
before it actually takes place. I'm glad we went for
it and that Ninja was aired the way we wanted, in
China and in other MTV regions.'

STAYING ALIVE CHINA CAMPAIGN:
NINJA, THE ENDURING MASTER

143

TITLE

MOBILE CHART

REGION

MTV ITALY

ARTIST

LORENZO BANAL

ATTITUDE: 'One for the money, two for the show.'
LOCATION: Milan, Italy
CLIENTS: MTV

CREDITS

DIRECTOR: Lorenzo Banal
MUSIC: Chicks on Speed

CONCEPT

'This job was specifically for MTV. The show is a chart for phone ringtones. The elements we wanted to focus on were music charts and the imagery of mobile phones, which gave us the idea of connecting a phone to some oversized amps. The graphic elements are there to provide dynamism.'

MAKING IT

'The 3D was intentionally minimal and stylized to provide coherence with the rest of the design. It took a week for the design work, and another week for compositing. 3D was done with Maja and compositing with Flint.'

ON AIR

'It works great on air and is still being aired a year later. The job was specifically for MTV Italia and I don't know if other regions use this package. For the past two years, my portfolio has consisted of only MTV work so, obviously, I think, MTV is the perfect client.'

MTV & OLA PRESENT SOLSTICE; A TRIBUTE TO THE SUMMER

MTV NETHERLANDS

TOKO / SHOP AROUND

ATTITUDE: 'We try to make a bridge between underground and commercial art. We'd like to think that we keep pace with what is happening around us and reflect that in our work.'
LOCATION: Rotterdam, the Netherlands
CLIENTS: MTV, TMF, The Box, Suzuki, Air Miles, Nickelodeon, BCC, Playboy, FFWD Heineken Dance, Parade, Endemol

MTV CREATIVE DIRECTOR: Danny Smit
REALISED BY: Toko at Shop Around

CONCEPT

'Solstice is an exclusive party, organised by MTV and the ice-cream manufacturer Ola to celebrate the longest day of the year. Since it was not a commercial party, MTV viewers could get on the guest list by entering the contest on MTV's website. So MTV Netherlands commissioned us to come up with a promotional film. In the brief we were asked to explain what Solstice was and create an uplifting promo that makes you long to be present on this hot summer night, filled with great performances like Amy Winehouse, Zuco 103 and many others.'

MAKING IT

'The main challenge on this project was to include a lot of information within 25 seconds (explaining what Solstice is, promoting a contest and listing the artist line-up), and still keep it entertaining and comprehensive. It took us about eight days from start to finish. We worked with Illustrator and After Effects and had some help from MCW with the technical implementation. In the end we learned that making promo films can be fun!'

ON AIR

'We have received a few compliments and have something good to put on our reel. Having the clip in our portfolio might have been the reason why we were asked to do the Station ID for the music channel TMF in the Netherlands and in Belgium, and this resulted in even more work for MTV. MTV is no different to other clients, it's all about the product and what counts is that it needs to be a good product. For this clip we had to use a certain style and also had to work with colours that were used for the Identity of the ice-cream brand, Ola.'

new

MTV emerging markets

alexandra Jugovic, Florian Schmitt

ATTITUDE: 'Everything we do is built on ideas and finding the most creative solution; and about having as much fun as possible while doing so.'
LOCATION: London, UK
CLIENTS: Lions Gate Entertainment, HBO, Mitsubishi Motors, Lexus Motors, Sony, Diesel Style Lab, Dentsu, Bacardi, Wieden & Kennedy

MTV HEAD OF PROGRAMMING AND PRODUCTION: Tanja Flintoff
DESIGN COMPANY: Hi-ReS! London
PRODUCERS: Kjetil Njoten/MTV, Tracey Bass/Hi-ReS!
DIRECTORS, DESIGNERS: Alexandra Jugovic, Florian Schmitt
CREATIVE DIRECTORS: Alexandra Jugovic, Florian Schmitt, Cam Levin/MTV
SOUND DESIGNER: Clifford Gilberto
POST-PRODUCTION: Blue, London
PRODUCER: Alison Wendt
FLAME ARTIST: Martin Goodwin
MUSIC: Clifford Gilberto

CONCEPT

'To come up with titles, set-, sound- and logo-design for one of MTVs most innovative shows, MTV:New. It was shot with five kids between the ages of three and eight and tons of flowers. Our concept was "twisted wonders", the amazement that you find in children's eyes when they see something for the first time, which is somewhere between being fascinated and being unsure. MTV approached us with a standard brief, which wasn't very specific in terms of creativity, just that it's a show that plays all the latest and best videos out there. They did, however, send us a tape with the previous design, so we could get an idea of what they had done before. As soon as we put the tape in the VCR, everyone crowded around the set, because the new Queens of the Stone Age video was playing and nobody had seen it before. I looked around and realised that this is what it's all about, curious faces, soaking up each pixel from the screen. And it reminded us of the way children see things for the first time, with a mixture of amazement, joy and a hint of uncertainty. So we started casting kids and ended up with five we thought would work, though not all of them made it into the final edit. We decided to mix it with exotic and somewhat alluring flowers to introduce a contrasting element and give the narrative a context.'

MAKING IT

'I guess the main challenge was to keep five kids happy and focused throughout a normal shoot day. Most of these kids are professionals, they do this kind of thing every week, but still, they're kids, and they are moody and get tired. It was really hot in the studio and we were filming on green screen, with no props, so they had to imagine what was around them. We had a one-day shoot, and about three days post-production, so it's one of the fastest jobs we ever made. All of the post-production was done in Flame, we did the offline in Final Cut and the final edit on the Flame as well. Working with the post-production house, Blue, on the piece, we learned that it's nice to be a client for once.'

ON AIR

'It was nice to see the whole package being used on-air, especially because we hadn't done anything like it before. We always wanted to work for MTV when we were students; trying to come up with elaborate plans to get our work shown; so actually getting a job was amazing. We have done other projects for them in the meantime and they are one of our favourite clients, mostly because they move so fast that they are not afraid to make mistakes. I think that liberates them and the people they work with and it shows in the work they commission.'

MTV VIDEO MUSIC AWARDS, BEST R&B VIDEO: POLVO

MTV US

LOBO

ATTITUDE: 'The constant objective of doing unique work every time around.'
LOCATION: São Paulo, Brazil
CLIENTS: Viva, Diesel, Panasonic, Sony Playstation, Boomerang Channel, Gessy-Lever, Toyota, Subaru, Cartoon Network, AnimeChannel, OLN, CMT, KesselsKramer, McCann Erickson, AMC, Ogilvy & Mather Worldwide, Saatchi & Saatchi, BBDO, MTV, Disney

MTV SVP ON AIR DESIGN AND OFF AIR: Jeffrey Keyton
MTV SVP ON AIR PROMOS: Kevin Mackall
CREATIVE DIRECTOR: Mateus de Paula Santos
ANIMATION: Marcos Llussá, Chico Sanches, Adriannus Cafeu
DESIGN: Carlos Bêla, Guilherme Marcondes, Cadu Macedo

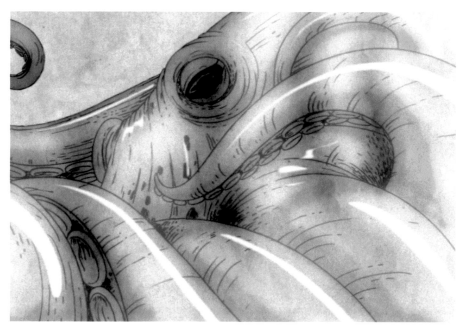

CONCEPT

'This was a promo for MTV's Video Music Awards, for the Best R&B Video category. We decided to show love among octopuses, since it needed to be kind of R&B sexy. It started out as an unintended pun. In a brainstorming meeting, someone suggested we did something showing people in love. The word "people" translates in Portuguese as "povo". Then someone else misunderstood that word for "polvo" which means octopus. We laughed and thought it could turn out cool.'

MAKING IT

'The difficult part was relating to the musical genres without being too straightforward or obvious. Also, the spot had to be predominantly black and white. We used a cell animation technique, which is not very common for the medium and is also very labour intensive which made it almost insane for our animators. We learned that a misunderstanding can generate an original idea, and that the post-production gave the cell animated octopuses a shiny-looking skin, and added interesting colour shades. We are very fond of mixing different techniques.'

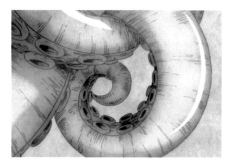

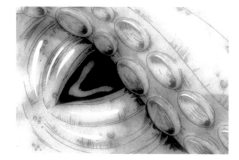

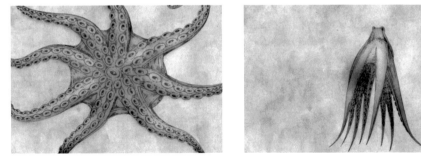

MTV VIDEO MUSIC AWARDS,
BEST R&B VIDEO: POLVO

TITLE

UP NORTH THE MUSIC TITLE SEQUENCE

REGION

MTV NORDIC

ARTIST

B-REEL

ATTITUDE: 'A new approach to every project.'
LOCATION: Stockholm, Sweden
CLIENTS: MTV, Forsman and Bodenfors, H&M, Swedish National Television, TV 4, Taivas, Kanal 5 and 3, Viasat Broadcasting, Ikea

CREDITS

MTV CREATIVE DIRECTOR: Lars Beckung
DIRECTOR: B-Reel
MUSIC PRODUCTION: Hector

CONCEPT

'MTV Nordic asked B-Reel to produce a new title sequence for the music segment "Up North". Our concept, of polar bears in an urban environment, is a paraphrase of the assumptions of non-Scandinavians, who sometimes believe that we actually do have polar bears running around our city centres. We also wanted to do something in line with a previous title sequence, for the earlier season, which featured penguins, who in fact by the way only live at the South Pole and not Up North at all. The abandoned, empty feeling of the clip makes the atmosphere dream-like and suggestive.'

MAKING IT

'The clip was produced in Photoshop and After Effects and the 3D animations were made in Maya. We use stills of different buildings and places in Stockholm, such as a multi-storey car park and the tax office. The most difficult part was getting the bears to move like we wanted.'

ON AIR

'This wasn't our first production for MTV and hopefully not our last. MTV always brings creative challenges and responds positively to edgy ideas.'

ANGEL: AHOGADO, GARGOLA, PESCADO

REGION

MTV LATIN AMERICA

ARTIST

MDL-MEDIALUNA

ATTITUDE: 'Never, ever, work overtime, the only good designers are the ones who sleep well. Have a nice team with no stars, no one is above the rest.'
LOCATION: Buenos Aires, Argentina
CLIENTS: MTV, TNT, Discovery Networks, VH1, Warner Channel, Nickelodeon, AXN, Cartoon Network, Playboy TV, Retro

CREDITS

MTV DIRECTOR, ON AIR:
Alejandro Abramovich
GENERAL MANAGERS: Javier Mrad,
Eduardo Maraggi
DESIGN, ANIMATION:
Fernando Vallejos, Sergio Saleh
PHOTOGRAPHY: Hernan Reig,
Xavier Martin
MUSIC: Sergio Vainikoff

CONCEPT

'We were hired by MTV Latin America for a three-spot ident campaign to be aired along with the channel's new image. We were asked to create the pieces in an urban environment, given the fact that it would be key for the channel's new image. So we came up with the idea of this young character caught in the middle of the city's modern life angst. To escape he becomes an angel so as to reach MTV's heaven, suffering different fates in each ident. We tried to reflect the feeling many of our friends were having at the time; of having no faith in the country and dreaming of reaching broadcast design heaven in MTV Miami.'

MAKING IT

'We started by out wandering around the city, with an actor improvising for three photographers who took over 800 pictures using 35mm film. Then we sort of threw all the pictures on the floor and started playing around with them until a few storyboards emerged. We then did a more careful selection, dividing the shots into two groups; the ones that would help us narrate the character actions, and the ones we would use to compose the urban sights. The offline was edited over an audio draft, which was then given to the musician so that he could create an original track that matched the offline's rhythm. We wanted the audio to build a hostile and disconcerting atmosphere. At the end, all the tension built up by the audio would disappear. That's why the soundtrack is built entirely by sound effects and only at the end can we hear a piece of music, which is intimately related to each ident's particular ending. Once the offline was approved, the photo compositions were defined and the overall image was adjusted whilse the musician worked on finishing touches to the soundtrack.'

ON AIR

'MTV makes you feel as if you were the client, they participate with good advice and allow a lot of freedom. It's a privilege for us to work for a channel like MTV, as we are part of a generation who used to run home after school to be dazzled by those strange-looking but beautiful audio-visual pieces in each commercial break, while watching our music idols. As time went by, those breaks were our only reason to turn on the television.'

ANGEL: AHOGADO, GÁRGOLA, PESCADO

PHASE R AND PHASE S, MTV ART BREAKS

MTV INTERNATIONAL

DANIEL HOLZWARTH

ATTITUDE: 'In a digital world there would be no more umlauts.'
LOCATION: Ludwigsburg, Germany
CLIENTS: MTV

MTV CREATIVE DIRECTOR: Cristian Jofre
DIRECTOR: Daniel Holzwarth

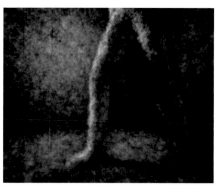

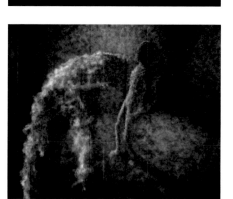

CONCEPT

Phase R: 'I was inspired for this by Japanese noise music. I wanted to make a spot about a world that is in constant change. The figure in the film is not able to orientate itself or to grab hold.'
Phase S: 'The inspiration for this was an old factory building that I visited with my video camera. It was basically an animation exercise as part of my film studies course. The original film is much longer.'

MAKING IT

Phase R: 'The greatest challenge was to create a new impression, a new look, using computer-animation tools. I learned that you can do much more with 3D animation than with photorealism or cartooning.'
Phase S: 'I always wanted to animate a figure executing a dance underwater. It was interesting working out how to animate atypical movements just out of my head; I had no instruction book or examples whilst I was making it. Each piece took about two weeks to make using PC, 3D and 2D software.'

ON AIR

'After seeing the spots on MTV, friends of mine are constantly talking to me about them. MTV sent me a photo from New York where my spots were showing simultaneously on the biggest outdoor screen in the world in Times Square.'

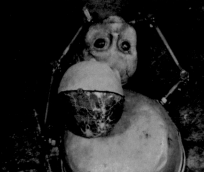

TITLE

MUDA,
ESFERA,
MTV ART BREAKS

REGION

MTV INTERNATIONAL

ARTIST

LUIS FELIPE HERNANDEZ
ALANIS

ATTITUDE: 'I am looking for my own personal style, far away from dominant visual culture and artistic clichés.'
LOCATION: Morelos, Mexico
CLIENTS: MTV

CREDITS

MTV CREATIVE DIRECTOR: Cristian Jofre
DIRECTOR: Luis Felipe Hernandez Alanis
MUSIC: Manuel Guerra

CONCEPT

'These Art Breaks are fragments from two different short films that I made, so the pieces came before the commission. The transition into MTV Art Breaks was interesting because I could only show a small part of each film but it had to be strong enough to stand up for itself and be self-contained.
Esfera: This sequence shows a boy confronting a sculpture dedicated to human fertility. The boy compares this image with a picture of his mother and also a picture of a religious figure.
Muda: This short is about when a baby is born, about the way that baby is completely vulnerable in the world.'

MAKING IT

'Both these short films were made with home-made materials and equipment; a very cheap cybershot, models made from garbage and pieces improvised for stop motion. Muda was made without any prior knowledge of stop-motion animation and without knowing anything about armatures, aluminium wire or software for capturing. That's why I used these sorts of materials. It took about six months to make each one. No one helped me with the shorts, only with the music. I learned a lot technically, better than at any school, about control, time and puppet motion. Artistically I learned to be a part of a piece, to feel life running through my fingers and to be transported into a piece, it was very exciting.'

ON AIR

'MTV is one of the best clients for people like me because they are very open. The restrictions were minimal, really different from a client who likes to tell you the exact Pantone colour and size for their logo. Having this work in my portfolio is helpful for presenting myself as an artist, and MTV is respected by advertising and media companies. I haven't actually had the occasion to pitch for a job saying that I worked for MTV, but for trying to get financial support for my short films I think it really helps. The impact of having my work shown on a big media channel around the world is very significant for me. I grew up watching Art Breaks in the 1990s and I loved them. Now being on the other side of the screen is very exciting. Also having the opportunity to show my work to people all over the world, from Japan to Brazil, is amazing.'

FARMING THE FUTURE

MARK TUNGATE

Soon, very few people will just sit back and watch television. The range of alternative media platforms is becoming too wide and too compelling to ignore. Spurred on by this digital revolution, MTV is constantly exploring services that enable its consumers to access content whenever, wherever and however they want to.

'Digital media is one of our key creative priorities,' confirms Brent Hansen, President of Creative & Editor in Chief, MTV Networks International and president, MTV Networks Europe. *'Technological developments, from mobile to broadband, interactive television, games and beyond, enable us to create deeper relationships with our audiences.'*

MTV is now a channel only in the broadest sense of the term. In the words of Jason Hirschhorn, senior vice president, Digital Music and Media, MTV Networks, it's more *'a youth entertainment portal'.*

While many media companies are still struggling to absorb the fact that passive television viewing is no longer the only option, MTV has been quick to embrace the possibilities of interactive television. In the UK and Ireland alone, it has been in the interactive space since early 2002, when MTV Hits launched a 24 hour interactive service on Sky Digital. Quizzes, customised screen environments and the ability to vote for favourite tracks all brought viewers into the action.

This was followed by the launch of an interactive service on MTV UK. Here, too, viewers can take part in interactive competitions, and vote artists on and off the MTV playlist. Every time their favourite artist appears on screen, they can access the latest news and gossip about their idol. New additions to the service seem to emerge almost every day.

Another form of interactivity is an innovation called Peep MTV. This 'best of MTV' destination gives viewers the chance to select their preferred content. When they enter Peep MTV, they see four preview screens. By pressing 'select', viewers can enlarge whichever screen they like the look of, depending on whether they're in the mood for news,

exclusive videos, archived and upcoming MTV programming, or rare and quirky content from MTV and elsewhere.

Interactive television is just the tip of the digital iceberg. The channel has long provided its fans with a comprehensive online service available in 37 localised URL versions. But now it can integrate the power of the web with the possibilities of broadband. Its first broadband service, MTV Live, launched in 2001 and is currently available in five markets (the UK, the Netherlands, Belgium, Norway and Italy), with others to come. It features on-demand video content, news, live events and MTV-created games. More recently, in 2005, MTV Italy launched a video-on-demand service in partnership with Telecom Italia. This subscription-based service enables users to build a playlist of videos and other music content, such as live performances, and then stream it to their PCs. A mobile version of the service went live in the same year.

The USA is highly advanced when it comes to broadband. Launched in 2005, MTV Overdrive is an interactive hybrid network. In other words, it's online television in its slickest form. Jason Hirschhorn explains; *'MTV Overdrive enables viewers to lean back and watch content in a more traditional way, or lean in and define what they want.'*

Viewers can mix and match news, music, behind-the-scenes reports from popular MTV shows, movie trailers and star interviews, among other ingredients. Overdrive also offers access to original online programming, such as the exclusive MTV.com Live performance series. Hirschhorn adds; *'By giving viewers the chance to create the television station they want, Overdrive makes the words "I want my MTV" a reality. We're seeing the evolution of MTV into an ecosystem in which we hand you the content, and you decide how to experience it. The satisfaction you get out of that is attributable back to the brand.'*

Young consumers increasingly spend more time with their cell phones than in front of the television, so MTV isn't neglecting the wireless generation.

Certainly, MTV is already here on your phone . Via deals with Hutchison and Vodafone, 3G mobile phone users in Europe can download MTV News clips, live performances and clips of popular shows. Viewers in France and Spain have access to a range of mobile MTV services. In Germany, mobile users can buy an MTV pre-paid content card from national retail outlets. Sophisticated 3G video services are available in the United States and even in China. MTV Music Zone, a subscription music service, is available via China Mobile, giving no less than 200 million users potential access to MTV music charts and entertainment news.

One of the most striking wireless developments is MTV Load, which sprang out of MTV's global partnership with Motorola. Launched in 2005 across Europe, MTV Load is an integrated on-air, mobile and WAP initiative. Humorous animations and live action programming are aired across MTV's European network, and can be downloaded by MTV viewers to their mobiles, free of charge.

Henrik Werdelin, vice president, Strategy and Product Development, MTV Networks International, comments; *'Mobile communications is something we believe in because our audience has embraced it; the mobile phone is this generation's device. And because it's a personal device, it enables us to become much closer to them.'*

MTV Load content has been created by leading art directors, animators and graphic illustrators around the world. An MTV Load website, localised for each market, acts as a 'shop window' for content. Users enter their telephone number to receive an automatic WAP URL, which gives them access to wallpapers, skins, ringtones, screensavers and entertaining short vignettes. *'One thing that we mustn't forget when we're talking about technology is that it allows creative people to tell stories in new ways'*, Werdelin observes. He points out that technology is narrowing the gap between entertainment provider and audience; to such an extent that it will soon disappear. *'MTV will generate platforms where kids can create their own content and deliver it to us, so we can share it with others.'*

If proof were needed, MTV has already published an online magazine created by its own readers. *MTV: Starzine* came about when Nokia approached the channel with the idea of delivering a project that took inspiration from blogging, but with an MTV twist. In order to secure space in the magazine, viewers were invited to 'snap, send and shine'. They would snap photographs on their mobile phones, send them to the *MTV: Starzine* website via MMS (or computer upload), and 'shine' by placing the photographs in the context of their own magazine pages. Participants could view all of the pages and vote online for their favourites; the most popular then went 'live'.

Cristián Jofré, senior vice president, creative director, MTV Networks International, points out; *'Over the last ten years, our viewers have evolved into users. They no longer just want to watch, they want to upload, download, customise and create; and we need to reflect that. I'm sure it's no coincidence that one of our most popular shows, 'Pimp My Ride', is all about customisation.'*

Another area of growing importance for MTV and its users is gaming. Over the past few years, MTV has been behind interactive TV games such as 'Ad Break Tennis' and 'Mugshot Mania' (which involved snapping celebrities in a virtual backstage environment). Games are now going mobile. In Germany a Pimp My Ride game is the number one game on T-Mobile. Following the official launch in 2005 of an MTV Games division, *'a dedicated gaming laboratory and interactive studio for the creation, incubation and development'* of new games, these initiatives are about to move onto a whole new level.

Japan has always been a crucible of futuristic entertainment, and many of MTV's developments there point the way to its digital future. For a start, it provides a diverse range of wireless services, streaming content to millions of users through operators KDDI and NTT DoCoMo. As well as producing bespoke entertainment content, MTV creates 'mini ads' for its advertising clients, linking them to the front and back end of content.

But perhaps the most interesting service in Japan is FLUX, an entirely new wireless brand concept. Described as 'the world's first mobile entertainment community', FLUX will gradually be launched in other markets around the world.

Tony Elison, senior vice president and general manager of Digital Media at Viacom International Japan, says; *'FLUX is a revolution in the literal sense of the word. Although MTV didn't invent cable television, we were among the first to figure out how best to use it to connect with consumers. FLUX is in exactly the same kind of spirit in the mobile environment.'*

Targeting 13- to 34-year-olds, FLUX offers access to original video and animation from Japan's leading names, as well as programming from the global MTV Networks library. To help launch the service, FLUX joined forces with Japanese pop sensation Utada (who has sold more than 37 million units) to produce the world's first music videos made exclusively for mobile phones. The Japanese animator Koji Morimoto created clips to illustrate tracks from Utada's release 'Exodus'.

The community element at the heart of FLUX provides an extra emotional dimension. Tony Elison explains; *'After watching something, you can recommend it to others by putting your name up on the screen. Other users can respond, make comments, and sharing their own recommendations. You end up creating pages of content in a mini-blogging experience.'*

Users who successfully 'promote' new FLUX content build up bonus points, giving them access to additional content, services or even products. *'In the future, you may be able to exchange FLUX points for a cappuccino'*, says Elison.

Access to FLUX costs the equivalent of three dollars a month, via KDDI Corporation's AU/EZWEB service.

FLUX is a good example of MTV's blend of creativity and commercial foresight. Brent Hansen explains; *'We're uniquely able to share expertise and innovations from markets such as Japan and Korea with our entire global network, which allows us to move quickly in developing breakthrough applications.'*

In the digital arena, as in others, MTV has proved skilled at inventing applications before its consumers even knew they wanted them – until they become hooked. Perhaps that's because, as Cristián Jofré says, *'the best way of predicting the future is to create it'.*

TITLE

SITARA

REGION

MTV INDIA

ARTIST

RUCHI PANDE,
MAYUR TEKCHANDANEY

ATTITUDE: 'We are creative because it's
the only thing we're good at.'
LOCATION: Mumbai, India

CREDITS

MTV VP CREATIVE AND CONTENT:
Cyrus Oshidar
DIRECTORS: Ruchi Pande,
Mayur Tekchandaney
PHOTOGRAPHER: Prasad Naik
ONLINE EDITOR: Prakash Kurup
OFFLINE EDITOR: Miten Udeshi
SOUND DESIGNER: Jiten Solanki
MUSIC: Ram Sampat, Derek

CONCEPT

'The idea was to package a block of back-to-back
songs of one particular Bollywood star. Every week
a different star would be featured. Sitara means
star in Hindi and was a popular adjective used to
describe past Bollywood stars. The still photos were
inspired by publicity shots from old Hindi films.
Each set-up jumps straight out of a Hindi film,
whether it's a cabaret number or a dream sequence,
a song in the Alps or an abrupt jig in the garden;
they are all reminiscent of these films. Music plays
an integral part in tying the visuals together as it
makes use of clichés rampant in Bollywood films.'

MAKING IT

'The shoot and post-production went quite smoothly on this project. We shot the stills on 35mm. The
prints were scanned and then worked on with
Smoke.'

ON AIR

'The clip was created for MTV India and was very
well received. In fact most of our clips have been
created for MTV India, so we do not really have the
perspective of working for other clients.'

HOUSEFULL
TUNE-IN

MTV INDIA

RUCHI PANDE,
MAYUR TEKCHANDANEY

ATTITUDE: 'We are creative because it's the only thing we're good at.'
LOCATION: Mumbai, India

MTV VP CREATIVE AND CONTENT:
Cyrus Oshidar
DIRECTORS: Ruchi Pande,
Mayur Tekchandaney
DOP: Amitabh Singh
PRODUCTION DESIGN: Swadha Kulkarni
OFFLINE: Yusuf
ONLINE: Prakash Kurup
MUSIC: Rajat Dholakia
SOUND DESIGN: Jiten Solanki

CONCEPT

'The film plays on the over-dramatic nature of most Bollywood films; especially during the 1970s and 1980s, several rags to the riches stories about abandoned or orphaned children trying to make it in the big bad world were released. In our promo, the boy's day gets progressively worse and ends in an anti-climax where the only joy in his life, Bollywood films, is stolen from him.'

MAKING IT

'As usual, budget was a problem; trying to achieve the scale of a Bollywood feature with limited means, from not affording to shoot the first sequence on location, to making the kids' disability credible. It was shot on 16mm.'

ON AIR

'There were mixed responses to this promo, most people got the joke, others were offended and thought it was insensitive to people with disabilities. It was taken off the air.'

VIDEOLOGIA PACKAGING

MTV LATIN AMERICA

PATTY ARANA

ATTITUDE: 'My true and honest self can only be seen through my work.'
LOCATION: Miami, USA
CLIENTS: Nickelodeon Latin America, MTV Latin America

MTV DIRECTOR, ON AIR:
Alejandro Abramovich
DIRECTOR: Patty Arana
RENDERINGS: Micaela Gonzalez
SOUND DESIGN: Juan Somarriba,
Andres Caceres
SOUND MIXING: Andres Caceres

CONCEPT

'This clip is part of a packaging done exclusively for MTV Latin America. The packaging was part of the channel's "Lightswitch", which happens every year and it involves the re-design and update of the channel's look. In this case, the packaging was done for an afternoon block called "Videología", which showcased vintage music videos from MTV's archives presented and discussed by some of the channel's VJs. The whole "Lightswitch" look had a very defined theme of urban chaos. That inspired me to search for personal representations of chaos in my environment. Where the chaos starts and ends on the streets, in cities, in buildings and social environments.'

MAKING IT

'The main challenge was to look for an original idea through which I could display my own view of urban chaos. My solution was to take it to a smaller scale, to a more personal, in-your-face interaction with the subject. This is why I used the interior of a regular house to examine how this environment could be a metaphor for what we perceive as urban chaos. The project took aproximately three weeks from concept to completion. Part of it is made from actual hand drawings and renderings, which were then brought into a 3D environment. Some 3D elements were added later; we used After Effects, Illustrator, and Lightwave for the digital compositing. At the beginning of the project my idea was to keep it a "hand drawn" piece and less digital. But we noticed there was no sense of space, something that would drive the viewer into the different stages of what I had in my mind. This is where the 3D came in and we split the hand paintings into different layers in a 3D space, adding a camera travel. Within the 3D

space the piece took on a more personal look, the viewer's point of view, and gave the project a kind of dramatic twist.'

ON AIR

'This piece was given a gold BDA award, which is great recognition and a personal reward. The On-Air team at MTV Latin America has earned many awards and recognition for different pieces related to this and other "Lightswitch" projects. This is one of many projects I did as part of the MTV Latin America On-Air team. The packaging was shown throughout the region. As challenging as it always is, no matter the size, time and budget, the freedom we are given to create and experiment is what makes these teams so successful.'

videología

TITLE

MTV EUROPE MUSIC
AWARDS 2001
MAIN TITLE SEQUENCE

REGION

MTV EUROPE

ARTIST

FRANÇOIS CHALET

ATTITUDE: 'I like simple ideas.'
LOCATION: Zürich, Switzerland
CLIENTS: MTV, Dalbin.com, OP Vodka,
Docomo, Mitsubishi, Expo 02, Fantoche,
Prima Linea, Centre Georges Pompidou

CREDITS

DIRECTOR: François Chalet
PRODUCER: Prima Linea Productions

CONCEPT

'One day I received a phone call from MTV UK who wanted me to pitch for a package. While working on the stage design, MTV took inspiration from my book "Chalet" [Die Gestalten Verlag, 2000]. I think the book was the reason they asked me to do the job in the first place. My idea was very simple. I put a giant turntable in the middle of a town (Frankfurt). The people of the town get affected by the music and stars and start running up to the turntable, which is the MTV European Music Awards. It's about BING! BANG! BOOM! – very superficial, weird, crazy, explosive.'

MAKING IT

'I'm used to working alone and doing all my animations on my own. This time, however, I decided to work with a handful of animators because of the amount we had to do in such a short time. So I worked with Prima Linea Productions in Paris. Everything was animated on Flash and the final edit was made on Final Cut. I was the director, but still animated as much as I could. But, we had almost finished the work on 11th September 2001 when the towers crashed. Frankfurt is known for being a little like New York so I had used a lot of tall buildings in the animation and people jumping out of windows. Obviously, the next day we got a phone call from MTV saying that we had to change everything that could be related to the crash. We could not have people jumping out of buildings. The houses couldn't have more than three floors and so on. It was a strange time, even more so because it suddenly became so strange to do this fun thing parallel to this horrific act. When I look back, I think it was good to go on with the show. Of course, in the end the animation was not as strong as I had planned, but that's life.'

ON AIR

Having MTV on your CV is a good thing! It was a great promotion for me and other clients followed. I had hardly any restrictions (only after the crash, but that's understandable). This job didn't make me rich, but it was really fun and useful promotion. After you have achieved a dream you think differently. It was like crossing a line and getting to the other side. Now I look at it in a little more relaxed way. It was a good time and I'm happy to work on other projects. I think a lot of people project their dreams onto MTV (as I did), but if you have lived this experience you see that MTV is a company, like any other. It has to make a lot of money. Their luck is that they can do it with things that are cool. It began underground and now it has become a huge industry; it's a process of evolution.'

ƎRBOL: ƎRT NOUVEƎU, ƎNEMONES, TRƎNSPORTƎTION

MTV LƎTIN ƎMERICƎ

MDL-MEDIƎLUNƎ

ATTITUDE: 'Never, ever, work overtime, the only good designers are the ones who sleep well. Have a nice team with no stars, no one is above the rest.'
LOCATION: Buenos Aires, Argentina
CLIENTS: MTV, TNT, Discovery Networks, VH1, Warner Channel, Nickelodeon, AXN, Cartoon Network, Playboy TV, Retro

MTV DIRECTOR, ON AIR:
Alejandro Abramovich
GENERAL MANAGERS: Javier Mrad, Eduardo Maraggi
DESIGN: Lorena Ruiz, Fernando Vallejos, Sergio Saleh, Federico Fabiano, Martín Shurmann
MUSIC: Sergio Vainikoff

CONCEPT

'MTV hired us to create a series of three idents. The idea was to work with trees and plants, to build a natural environment; relaxed, joyful. So we came up with three different approaches: In Anemones, we have a hopeful insight, seeing how discarded consumer goods become a place for life once thrown to the bottom of the sea. In Art Nouveau, we intended to give the audience a little break, a pause in the channel's constant rush of images. Transportation was the result of mapping a city onto a tree and looking for similarities, considering the urban landscape as a new natural world.'

MAKING IT

'Transportation was done in a week from start to finish , the other two took about three weeks.'

ON AIR

'These pieces won us several international awards, but what is even more satisfying is to see how an ident like Transportation can catch the audiences' eye and please the public.'

5 STAR
OPENING TITLES

MTV INTERNATIONAL

TANJA ADAMIETZ

ATTITUDE: 'My mission is to use my creative abilities to make a difference; to sensitise people.'
LOCATION: London, UK
CLIENTS: AOK, Armani, BBC, Campari, Lipton, MTV, Nike, Sony Ericsson, Staying Alive, Warsteiner

MTV CREATIVE DIRECTOR: Cristian Jofre
DIRECTOR: Tanja Adamietz
POST-PRODUCTION:
OnePost – Toby Abbott, Emma Watterson, Roisin, Martin Goodwin, Paul Sullivan
DESIGNER, ANIMATOR: Russ Murphy
MUSIC, SOUND DESIGN: Denis Ducasse

CONCEPT

'This piece is part of the title sequence for MTV 5 Star which is a branded artist franchise supported by all MTV International channels to promote new album releases. While designing the logo, the idea of creating an enchanted garden developed. I wanted to create a place where magic takes you into a new world. In this garden the animals are magic and always have five features, like the deer with the five ears. Album releases used to be an exciting event and I wanted to give some of the magic back. I also experimented with styles to archive a new visual world. I wanted to achieve a hyper-realistic world, an over-stylised paradise, almost kitsch; Goya meets a kebab shop!'

MAKING IT

'The biggest challenge was achieving the hyper-realist style. It was tricky to find a way of designing all the elements of the garden. I decided to use real footage instead of 3D, because neither the budget nor the time allowed for a full 3D-designed environment. The animals are live footage, additional features are tracked in After Effects. The backgrounds are a patchwork of different plants, flowers, waterfalls and clouds, etc. It was all created in Photoshop, animated in After Effects and put together in Flame. Effects like fog, clouds, mist and lightning were also put in later with Flame. It took around eight weeks from the first logo scratches to the final delivery of the title sequence. It is always an experiment to work with a group of different people, but luckily I found an excellent crew. Russ helped create the backgrounds in Photoshop, treating the animals and animating the scenes. Denis wrote a magical piece of music; and the post-production house, OnePost, did a great job in Flame and Infinity to finalise everything. It was a challenge for us all since none of us had done anything like this before, but we succeeded and were very happy with the result. This project made me realise how important an excellent crew is, people you can rely on and whom you trust.'

ON AIR

'In terms of feedback, I unfortunately don't know when the clip aired, but I did get asked by another MTV department to create the same kind of magical atmosphere for them. I worked for MTV as a Senior Producer and Designer for a couple of years. The absolute creative freedom I enjoyed during that time was phenomenal. I have never experienced it before, nor after, in my career. Experimentation and improvisation means mistakes and unconventional approaches, but offers an almost unlimited playground. I loved this crazy creative buzz! But MTV has grown into one of the biggest television networks of all time, which leaves less and less space to play. It is a crazy place to work!'

CLIP CLASSICS

MTV NETHERLANDS, MTV SCANDINAVIA

POSTPANIC

ATTITUDE: 'We are creative because we were never good at mathematics at school.'
LOCATION: Amsterdam, the Netherlands
CLIENTS: Nike, Sportlife, Deep, Miele, MTV, DSM, Ligaya / Gouryella

MTV CREATIVE DIRECTOR: Danny Smit
AGENCY: PostPanic
CREATIVE DIRECTORS: Mischa Rozema, Jules Tervoort, Mark Visser
DIRECTOR: Mischa Rozema
PRODUCER: Ania Markham
GRAPHICS, ANIMATION: Mischa Rozema, Jules Tervoort, Mark Visser

CONCEPT

'The clip was commissioned by Patrick Heerdink, Head of Creative at MTV NL, who we had worked with on other projects. He came up with an idea of using an archive theme for the new Clip Classics leader and asked us to develop it. We liked the idea of a family tree depicting every imaginable music style. So using a mixture of stills, motion graphics and 3D animation we created an ever-growing path of musical genres with a backdrop of a traditional museum interior that looks institutional.'

MAKING IT

'We had to produce a collection of stills of an existing museum archive and luckily we found one in Harlem that had just the right look and feel. The photo shoot took about a day and we spent just under two weeks creating and incorporating all the different graphic and animation elements together. The main tools we used were Illustrator, Photoshop and After Effects.'

ON AIR

'We would be lying if we said that we work for MTV purely for the money. As teenagers in the 1980s, MTV really inspired us and hence there's the buzz of creating work for such an iconic brand. However, the main appeal is the freedom they give you to carry out your own ideas. It's that freedom that allows you to go to places that would be deemed too risky or strange by many commercial clients. Take away that freedom of creativity and include more normality or conformity and working for MTV suddenly and sadly loses its appeal. All our work for MTV is regularly commented on and viewed with interest by our other clients. It allows them to see an edgier, raw side of PostPanic and provides an insight into other, less-commercial, directions

that our work can lead to. Clip Classics was commissioned for the Netherlands / Belgium market, however, MTV Scandinavia really liked it and decided to use it as well.'

TITLE

SPEAKERPLAY
PROMO

REGION

MTV BENELUX

ARTIST

CASPER BOERMANS

ATTITUDE: 'Creativity is about finding creative solutions. Computers or cameras are the tools for realising that solution.'
LOCATION: Utrecht, the Netherlands
CLIENTS: T-Mobile, Protest, X-Travel, MTV

CREDITS

MTV CREATIVE DIRECTOR: Danny Smit
MOTION DESIGN: Casper Boermans
ART DIRECTION, TEXT: Patrick Heerdink
AUDIO: J P van Druten
MUSIC: Miss Kitten

CONCEPT

'Patrick Heerdink, the art director, shot the footage with Miss Kitten and left me two days to create a promo of it. So I did not have much time to create a real concept.'

MAKING IT

'The swirl style is one of my favourites. I printed out the shots, bought some transparent sheets and started drawing swirls out of Miss Kitten. Then in After Effects I re-composed the video, made her clothes black and positioned her in the same place as for the paintings. Then I only had to animate the paintings and add them to the composition. When I finished I had to insert a bit more of the Speakerplay Festival artwork. So I made snapshots of their website and used some of the paintings as the background for the web graphics.'

ON AIR

'I've worked for MTV networks for three years now so this clip was not especially a big deal. In fact I have done much more spectacular work.'

SUPERMERCADO

MTV NORDIC

MANS SWANBERG / PISTACHIOS

ATTITUDE: 'Worn ideas give me a sinking feeling. So I avoid them, and voilà it's créatif!'
LOCATION: Stockholm, Sweden
CLIENTS: Sony Music, Harpers Bazaar, Wallpaper, Levi's, Edwin Jeans, Penguin Books, Cheap Monday, Tokion, Et Vous, MTV, Vogue Homme

MTV CREATIVE DIRECTOR: Lars Beckung
CONCEPT, ART DIRECTION, SOUND, ILLUSTRATION, ANIMATION: Pistachios

CONCEPT

'This started with Anna Källsen at MTV talking about singing mushrooms. We had some vague idea of a John Bauer-type forest, which was very much what it didn't turn out to be. The idea was to move through the forest with a sound coming closer, finally seeing the mushroom luring the logo out of the lake with his seductive chant. MTV wanted elements of the show (ie.games, fashion, movies) so we added those as well.'

MAKING IT

'The swirl pattern took over and turned into clouds, trees, water and volcanoes. It involved loads of tracing paper and scanning. The scenes are 3D planes with drawings mapped onto them. I played the melody on a theremin, and processed it into vocals using a vocoder.'

ON AIR

'There was a lot of good feedback. This clip had an impact on us in so far as we rediscovered what fun drawing is.'

THE TALKING BEAR

MTV BRAZIL

ANA STARLING

ATTITUDE: 'Looking at things and distorting their original meaning.'
LOCATION: São Paulo, Brazil

MTV PROMO MANAGER: Rodrigo Pimenta
DIRECTOR: Ana Starling

CONCEPT

'My inspiration for this particular piece came from a brainstorming session at MTV after I was hired to create a new identity for MTV in 2004. The idea was to create a product where mutation, replacement of things and distortion played key roles. I was free to create anything I wanted and came up with the idea of experimenting with surrealism. There is a mixture of elements in the clip; a fan producing real leaves or a bear with a human head that can talk.'

MAKING IT

'The female character, Joana, who is the bear's head, already existed at MTV. Since the idea was to keep her as part of MTV's identity the challenge was to build new packaging for her so that she would still draw people's attention. The whole process took about a month. My biggest problem was that I'd never done any animation work for TV before! I had to learn it overnight along with the responsibility of having to come up with something good. I did it all on my own using a Mac. Whilst making the clip I learnt that a piece of animation really depends on your concept as much as the elements in it. If you understand what the animation is all about you can make it; use any simple, basic resources and come up with great visual results.'

ON AIR

'The feedback was surprising. The audience recognised Joana and warmed to her. People wanted to know who had created the clip. This particular work was for MTV São Paulo and was aired all over the country. Working for MTV provides us with both visibility and the possibility of creating our own work. Most of my other clients already have an idea in mind when they approach me.'

TITLE

ALERT

REGION

MTV ASIA

ARTIST

LOBO

ATTITUDE: 'The constant objective of doing unique work every time around.'
LOCATION: São Paulo, Brazil
CLIENTS: Viva, Diesel, Panasonic, Sony Playstation, Boomerang Channel, Gessy-Lever, Toyota, Subaru, Cartoon Network, AnimeChannel, OLN, CMT, KesselsKramer, McCann Erickson, AMC, Ogilvy & Mather Worldwide, Saatchi & Saatchi, BBDO, MTV, Disney

CREDITS

MTV DIRECTOR, ON AIR PROMOTIONS, CREATIVE AND CONTENT: Charmaine Choo
CREATIVE DIRECTOR: Mateus De Paula Santos
DESIGN, ANIMATION: Cadu Macedo

CONCEPT

'This was a package for a show sponsored by Motorola for MTV Asia, Singapore. Since the show was related to a cellular phone brand, it was supposed to look urban and high-tech. The brief was very open, leaving the solutions to us; it also had to finish on a beacon so we decided to put it on top of a building. We had a very tight deadline to come up with the concept and produce all the package's elements. It was difficult since the pressure was high and it was one of our first experiences working outside the Brazilian market. The idea was based on a wild flying camera, looking for the source of light rays shining along the city skyline. The alert theme lead us to a light alert siren, which we thought was visually promising.'

MAKING IT

'We created a complete, compelling package with an open, bumpers, looped backgrounds, and so on. Probably the highlight of the project was the camera work; also, the simplified colour palette added to the overall look of the package. It was one of the first 3D spots we did entirely on a Mac platform with the early versions of Maya for the Mac.'

ON AIR

'There's one shot we're particularly fond of, a camera following an elevator going down. That required a lot of fine-tuning, and we feel it worked.'

La Cresta
Show Package

MTV Latin America

MK12

ATTITUDE: 'The work we create is a collective pastiche of our individual interests, influences, and styles, mashed together and reinvented as a single creative channel.'
LOCATION: Kansas City, USA

MTV DIRECTOR, ON AIR:
Alejandro Abramovich
DIRECTOR: MK12

CONCEPT

'MTV's La Cresta: A travelling rainbow is our friendly host through a colourful world of flowers, hidden treasure, and fresh beats. Our design for the show packaging was inspired by; My Little Pony©, pirates, mermaids and rainbows. We created an abstract landscape art-piece in Illustrator as a guide for the general look and feel of the environment, then pulled it apart and used pieces of it to create a 3D representation of the original work.'

MAKING IT

'It was hard work creating an entirely fictitious world from scratch in a short amount of time. The full project took us a little over a month working on Mac G3s. We developed the project in anticipation of After Effects 4.0's new 3D engine. When the software was finally released, there were a lot of bugs, and it didn't run as well as we had expected.'

ON AIR

'Feedback from this piece was very positive, as it was a new direction for us, visually speaking, and perhaps a bit lighter than our previous work. The feedback helped us realise that we were capable of exploring styles and techniques that we hadn't previously thought to combine, and that our audience was equally receptive to this new-found flexibility. Having MTV as portfolio work is always a milestone for motion-graphic designers; MTV was one of the first networks to be receptive to motion graphics as a promotional medium, and many designers got their start designing channel IDs and show packages for them. Generally speaking, MTV is respectful of the artists they work with, and therefore more unfiltered creative work makes it to air. For us, working with MTV caught the attention of other television networks, which in turn helped us get new work. MTV realises that to be successful as a network, it is important to always stay ahead of the curve, both with the music they expose and the designers who help develop their identity. MTV has always been a source for the new and unseen; for that reason, creative freedom is both allowed and encouraged.'

MTV VIDEO MUSIC AWARDS JAPAN 2005, EYEDOLL DISCOVERY HUNT

MTV JAPAN

KESSELSKRAMER

ATTITUDE: 'The quality of ideas, the challenge of working in new media, and the linking of interested people and thinking is at the core of the company's work in communication.'
LOCATION: Amsterdam, the Netherlands
CLIENTS: Bavaria Breweries, Absolut Vodka, Hans Brinker Budget Hotel Amsterdam, Diesel, Oxfam International, Trussardi, Ben Mobile Telephone Network, The City of Amsterdam, SNS Bank, Unilever

MTV EXECUTIVE PRODUCER ON AIR PROMOS AND CREATIVE: Miyako Hattori
STRATEGY: Engin Celikbas / KesselsKramer
CREATIVE: Tyler Whisnand, Nils-Petter Lövgren / KesselsKramer
PRODUCTION: Pieter Leendertse / KesselsKramer
ANIMATION: Fido, Stockholm
DOLL DESIGN: Jakob Westman, Arno Peters
SOUND DESIGN: Plopp, Stockholm

CONCEPT

'For the MTV Video Music Awards Japan 2005, MTV EyeDolls were placed all over Tokyo, turning the city into a scavenger hunt. KesselsKramer produced a series of commercials that served as announcements and clues as to where to find the MTV EyeDolls and therefore as an instrument for communication. The EyeDolls were made in five different colours. Each represented a different prize category that included sponsors such as Tommy Hilfiger, Apple iPod and Tower Records. MTV Japan asked for communication that would be surprising and engaging for young MTV viewers and extremely visible around Tokyo. We thought the EyeDoll would be something young people would like to have and keep. The story was that the EyeDolls escaped from MTV, so we created an animation that showed the EyeDolls literally popping out of the MTV Video Music Awards Japan 2005 logo.'

MAKING IT

'There were several challenges. The first was to arrange the design and proper manufacture of the MTV EyeDoll in five different colours. We scoured the planet to find the right person to help us. Once produced, the next challenge was to get them to Tokyo in time to have a good place for the scavenger hunt, and have the animation film ready at the same time. Fido and KesselsKramer worked round the clock. To shoot the clue idents in and around Tokyo posed an additional challenge and only the cooperation of MTV and KesselsKramer meant that the idents were ready on time. Budget and time constraints kept everyone drinking lots of coffee. All the television commercials were assembled and edited in Sweden and brought to MTV Japan where finished. The project was a multi-layered event; scavenger hunt, promotional activity and brand-building effort that combined different media and expertise.'

ON AIR

'For MTV Japan the results of the MTV EyeDoll Discovery Hunt were excellent. They received an increased amount of awareness for the Video Music Awards Japan 2005 and the EyeDolls became a much-loved item among viewers and fans. The Discovery Hunt lasted for one month and the build-up to the final weeks was particularly strong. The final silver EyeDolls were available in the last week and besides providing free admission to the award show, they also gave the lucky finder a chance to walk down the red carpet alongside the stars. MTV is an interesting client with a strong history and high brand recognition. It is a cultural institution in many ways. Working with MTV Japan was a challenge and we couldn't have done the job without the help of some key people who were instrumental in the progress of the project. There is a huge potential for doing relevant and social projects for MTV and we hope KesselsKramer will somehow take part in future initiatives both in Japan and Europe.'

TITLE

MTV HIJACK

REGION

MTV INTERNATIONAL

ARTIST

PRECURSOR

LOCATION: London, UK
CLIENTS: MTV, Nike, Channel 4, Sony, Emap, Orange, Five, Mute Records, Kudos Records, Ministry of Sound

CREDITS

MTV CREATIVE DIRECTOR: Cristian Jofre
DESIGN, DIRECTION,
2D AND 3D ANIMATION: Precursor
SOUND DESIGN, PRODUCTION: Si Begg

CONCEPT

'The theory behind our approach was based on MTV's perceived ownership of youth culture and the fact that they encompass so much more than music. We pulled together a huge amount of contemporary, and not so contemporary, cultural references and this notion of hijacking, of taking something that already exists and creating something new from it, seemed to be perfect for MTV. Everything from bootlegging, pirate radio, stickering, postering, graffiti, customised clothing, customised cars, adbusters, through to the Chapman Brothers and Christo, these were all points of reference for hijack. It is also a great word, very provocative. We created a new on-air identity based around this idea. The great thing about the project was that we wanted what we delivered to be hijacked, to be changed and developed and to evolve over time. The on-air look has been taken on by loads of countries internationally and in each region it looks slightly different, as it has absorbed cultural references from those countries.'

MAKING IT

'I think the main challenge with this project was working within a very tight budget for what was planned. We shot on film in three locations with a cast of three and then spent a lot of time on graphics after the shoot. Of course, idents and blips are only the tip of the iceberg on channel identity projects. There are a lot of other elements to create and deliver too, such as clip titles, promo endboards and style guides for on screen text. One problem we encountered was when we shot on the bus; we couldn't get the crane in there without taking out the front window, and the budget wasn't there for that. We eventually got the shot by dragging the producer's son's skateboard out of the van and using

it as a mini dolly on a board laid across the bus seats. We shot all three locations in London in one day with a small crew. All post work was done in-house at Precursor.'

ON AIR

'We had great feedback from this project and it has had a few column inches dedicated to it too, which is always good. MTV, as a client, allows a certain amount of freedom to experiment, which you may not get with some other clients. With the Hijack project, we were experimenting and messing around with elements until the final day. MTV International commissioned the project and it now airs across quite a few regions. Part of our stipulation when we delivered the project was that the nature of the idea was that it shouldn't end there. What we had produced shouldn't just be delivered on tape and then put straight on air. We encouraged regions to experiment with it, to hijack it further. We delivered a DVD full of drawings, animations and imagery that could be used as inspiration or as a starting point to take the project further.'

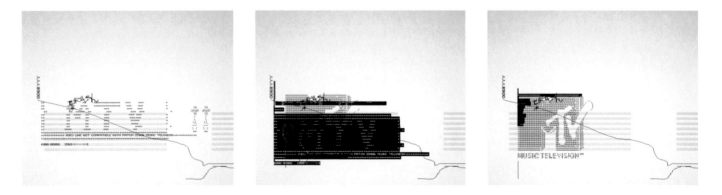

TITLE

MTV UK CHANNEL IDENTITY

REGION

MTV UK

ARTIST

SWEDEN GRAPHICS

ATTITUDE: 'Not to make interesting graphic design, but to make graphic design interesting.'
LOCATION: Stockholm, Sweden

CREDITS

MTV HEAD OF CREATIVE: Georgia Cooke
REALISED BY: Sweden Graphics

CONCEPT

'Our brief was to make a new channel identity for
MTV UK. Usually this kind of project consists of
three different types of material.

1. Graphics that are shown during ordinary shows,
such as the title board with the name of the music
video currently playing, text with information
about upcoming shows etc. These graphics are
mixed with the background image in the broadcast, alongside text information which is created
separately, since the content constantly changes.

2. Graphics shown in between shows. These graphics are stand-alone, since there is no background
image to mix with, but the text content still has to
be changeable and mixed with the graphics.

3. Idents, which are short image films that are
totally stand-alone with no changeable features.
This is the type that perhaps is most responsible
for MTV's visual fame. We wanted to create a concept that would make the difference between these
types less noticeable. We also felt that showing
text on a white rectangular shape is the best, most
straightforward way to display information on television. We hate bullshit graphics and always avoid
sacrificing function for style. So it came naturally
to us to let the graphics, as in type, be simple and
unobstructed and to make the white rectangle interesting. We made up a kind of creature called a
creeper, whose job it was to crawl around over the
screen and act as white background signs for whatever text information was needed. We did a whole
set up of different animations of creepers moving
over the screen and folding out into signs of different shapes and sizes. These animations are stored
digitally and can be used by the programming schedulers at any time during the shows. Text is also for-
matted individually for every creeper so that the
schedulers can type in any text information that

is needed. This worked as the type-1 graphics mentioned above. But we also needed to create type-2
graphics that could be used in-between commercial breaks. We wanted to use the creepers for this
as well, and since there is no background that the
creepers could crawl over we created a sort of MTV
off-stage area that the creepers could occupy when
they are not working on the shows. We built a set
in a studio and filmed a lot of footage of this area.
Then we animated creepers hurrying about in this
setting. Some creepers where animated to fold out
as signs for information about upcoming shows.
We also did animations of the creepers leaving the
screen, entering the off-stage area and thus creating a seamless transition between the type-1 and -2
graphics. All this material is also stored digitally
and the short clips are edited together randomly by
the broadcasting software, following some rules we
set up, into an endless variety of sequences. There
is also a setup of different background sounds that
are played randomly during the sequence. For the
idents we just made extra events happen within
the off-stage area as the creepers pass through
it. We felt that there was no good reason for using
the MTV logo here so we came up with a sonic logo
instead. According to MTV this is the first time in
the music channels history that MTV has produced
idents without showing the MTV logo.'

MAKING IT

'Probably the biggest challenge was to get everything to work technically. Luckily that was mostly
MTV's problem, not ours. Other than that, once we
came up with the concept and the way all the pieces
would fit together it was quite difficult fun work.
In all it took about six months to realise this project.
We did most of the work ourselves, but got help
with the carpentry, lighting, sound and the post-

production. The problems we encountered were
mostly due to the technical limitations of the broadcasting hardware. The technology was quite new to
MTV UK so there was a lot of trial and error to go
through.'

ON AIR

'We were nominated for the D&AD awards for this
work. Apart from that there are no concrete results, yet. Personally I am a bit disturbed when client lists are used as a sign of excellence but the
truth is that it undeniably makes a difference. As a
potential client you would be reassured that you
are hiring someone that can and will deliver, which
is a very important quality from the client's point
of view. Our experience with the people we worked
with at MTV is that they were more concerned and
knowledgeable in design matters than the average
client. Also I think that MTV is a client that is looking for design as an end in itself, which can be a
very favourable position if you know what you
want to do. Design awareness is an important part
of their brand and from the designer's point of
view that can mean that there is room for personal
expression. We felt very unrestricted, but we rarely
try to offend with our design. Some of our material
did not pass the regulations for epilepsy safety, but
other than that we only discussed design matters
with the client, never the content.'

TITLE

GIFTED

REGION

MTV US

ARTIST

LIFELONG FRIENDSHIP SOCIETY

ATTITUDE: 'We thrive on a kind of personal anarchy that translates into a larger freewheeling whole. We vibe on contradiction, juxtaposition, abstraction and detouring.'
LOCATION: New York, USA
CLIENTS: Favourite Sons, Gorochow, CTDMV, Smilefaucet, Carentan, McNees Wallace and Nurick, Sazaby, Tokyo, The Stitchery, Design is Kinky, Yuuki Ono, New Industry Standard, Mother NY

CREDITS

MTV SVP ON AIR DESIGN AND OFF AIR:
Jeffrey Keyton
MTV SVP ON AIR PROMOS: Kevin Mackall
DIRECTOR: Lifelong Friendship Society

CONCEPT

'MTV approached us with probably the best creative brief you could have from a client. They wanted the channel MTV Hits to be re-branded but they gave us free rein to do whatever we wanted; the only caveat being that it had to appeal mainly to girls within the 12 to 17 age group. MTV Hits is a mostly unmanned channel that plays to the TRL crowd, it's pure candy. They asked for six generic opens, various bumps and logo treatments that would serve as channel identification.'

MAKING IT

'We came up with a few different directions for MTV to choose from. Before pitching them we realised that while all three were visually different from each other, they shared a dimension of confrontation or involvement with the viewer. The one concept that did this the best was also the one that MTV chose to move forward with. It took about a month from concept to completion; about two weeks of which was pure production and animation. We shot it ourselves in the studio on DV in front of a green screen using our friends as cast. The lighting was a bit difficult but we figured it out in the end. The only help we really received was in mastering the audio; although we created the tracks ourselves, we felt it was necessary for them to be cleaned and synced and filled in a bit and we went to Nutmeg Audio Post for that. We always learn something about ourselves on a job; how we work and the process. With this one we realised that the DIY thing is really precious to us.'

ON AIR

'Feedback has been great. It was a very warm project all around. It's always a hurdle to realise that what you have just done will be something that people peg you as being, even if you have moved on a bit, or a lot, from it; in this case it's not bad. Of course we have moved on, but we were happy with the end result so it does inform some of our current work. MTV is a different beast from almost every other client. It has a propensity for allowing real left-field thinking in order to gain the attention of its audience. This works well for us too. The only real restrictions placed on us were who it needed to appeal to; that it couldn't be too violent, or male-oriented, not too aggressive, no gore, no sex.'

MTV STYLE AWARDS CHINA 2003 SHOW OPENER

MTV CHINA

KUOYU ANDREW LO

ATTITUDE: 'When one finds a different solution, I consider that creative.'
LOCATION: Beijing, Taipei, London
CLIENTS: MTV Networks International, MTV Asia Networks, MTV China, MTV Taiwan, Channel [V] Taiwan, Music Labels

MTV SUPERVISING PRODUCER, HEAD OF ON AIR PROMOS: Andrew Lo
DIRECTOR: Kuoyu Andrew Lo
PRODUCTION: Key Point Productions, Shanghai
ANIMATION: Bill Chia
MUSIC: DJ Shiuan, Taiwan

CONCEPT

'This opening sequence was part of the Style Awards campaign when MTV was launched in China in 2003. The brief was to design the entire campaign, from creative to final product, in two months.'

MAKING IT

'I had to fly back to Taiwan for this because at the time I was more confident working with production crews there. And with a timeframe like that I had no choice but to work with the best people.'

ON AIR

'The head of MTV's media partner in China actually came to shake my hand after the show. Do I sound like I'm exaggerating? Having this spot in my reel totally helps. It not only won a few awards, but as an opening of a popular award show in China, ratings in some cities can reached "6". Do you know how many people that is?!!'

ROAD TRIP

MTV SOUTH FEED

LORENZO BANAL

ATTITUDE: 'I like short songs.'
LOCATION: Milan, Italy
CLIENTS: MTV

DIRECTOR: Lorenzo Banal
MUSIC: Mad Zoo featuring Rosy Aragão

CONCEPT

'The job was made for MTV. The show is a travel diary of a VJ's trip around Europe. The main concept was a map, on which a path develops throughout with forks and junctions, strolling about and the unexpected. The colours and graphics remind me of a camping sticker that used to be on my parents' caravan that they had during the seventies.'

MAKING IT

'The artwork was produced in vector paths and animated with Flint. Shapes are geometrically regular to reflect the style of the urban grid. 3D layers were used in post-production to give a feeling of depth. The artwork drawings took a couple of days to produce, as did the compositing.'

ON AIR

'It works great on air and is still being aired a year later. The job was specifically for MTV Italia and I don't know if other regions use this package. For the past two years, my portfolio has consisted only of MTV work so, obviously, I think, MTV is the perfect client.'

MTV MASH
TITLES AND PACKAGING

MTV EUROPE

RUSS MURPHY

ATTITUDE: 'To make something better than last time.'
LOCATION: London, UK
CLIENTS: MTV, EMI Records, Channel 4, BBC1, Roughtrade Records, VH1

DIRECTOR: Russ Murphy
SOUND DESIGN: Jim Griffin

CONCEPT

'This is the main title sequence for the show "MTV Mash", a magazine-style show featuring various bootleg mixes...music mashed together. It was inspired by Lodown Magazine and was a direct commission from MTV that took three weeks to make.'

MAKING IT

'We made the sequence using a digital camera, a Mac G4, After Effects, Photoshop and Illustrator. The hardest part was trying to create a 3D line that drew itself on screen. I had a friend gather photos of urban environments that I used as backgrounds. A tip to anyone working with After Effects; always pre-comp when you can, no matter how tempting it is to build everything in one comp.'

ON AIR

'There has been a good response to the clip and it has brought me more work.'

Matt Hanson

Matt Hanson is a leading authority and expert in the field of digital moving image and emerging film futures. Screen International cited him as an international film visionary in a UK top ten including Mike Figgis, Ridley Scott, and Christopher Nolan, for his groundbreaking work in digital film. He has produced and commissioned over 40 digital films, and created two TV series on digital filmmakers. He founded the pioneering onedotzero digital film festival, and is the author of *The End of Celluloid*. He lives in Brighton, England.

Anne-Celine Jaeger

A regular contributor to *The Times*, *Design Week*, *Wallpaper* and *Neon*, Anne-Celine Jaeger specialises in lifestyle, art and design journalism. Writing in English and German, for a number of publications in the UK, America and Germany, she often documents stories with her own photography. Fluent in English, German, French and Italian, publications rely on her to interview people in their native tongue to get the better story. Based in London, Anne-Celine Jaeger works out of Milk Studios, a creative co-op, just off the Portobello Road.

Sophie Lovell

Sophie Lovell is a British writer and editor based in Berlin. She is the Germany editor for *Wallpaper* magazine and Architecture and Design editor for the German design magazine Qvest. Her work has also been published in *The Independent on Sunday*, *Interior Design*, *Time Out* and Birkhäuser Verlag. She has collaborated on numerous projects for Die Gestalten Verlag including writing the book *This Gun is for Hire*. She is also a consultant for Winkreative in London.

Mark Tungate

Mark Tungate is a British journalist and author based in Paris. He is a regular correspondent for *Campaign* magazine and writes a weekly column, Media Planet, for the French communications journal *Stratégies*. His work has appeared in *The Times* and *Telegraph* newspapers. He also contributes to the trend forecasting service Worth Global Style Network. He is the author of the books *Media Monoliths: How Great Media Brands Thrive and Survive*, and *Fashion Brands: Branding Style from Armani to Zara*, both published by Kogan Page.

ON AIR

✦ ✦

EDITED BY: Robert Klanten, Birga Meyer, Cristián Jofré
TEXT EDITOR: Sophie Lovell

WRITERS: Matt Hanson, Anne-Celine Jaeger, Sophie Lovell, Mark Tungate
LAYOUT AND DESIGN: Birga Meyer, Thorsten Geiger
ART DIRECTION: Robert Klanten
PRODUCTION MANAGEMENT: Martin Bretschneider
DVD PRODUCTION: Sven Haeusler
LEGAL ASSISTANCE: Jens Fischer
RESEARCH: Sven Ehmann
RESEARCH ASSISTANCE: Asia Kornacki
PROOFREADING: Liz Farrelly

Title font 'NormaleV2' was created by Atelier télescopique, Lille.

Published by Die Gestalten Verlag, Berlin 2005
ISBN 3-89955-061-7

Printed by Graphicom Srl, Vicenza
Made in Europe.

Bibliographic information published by Die Deutsche Bibliothek
Die Deutsche Bibliothek lists this publication in the Deutsche Nationalbibliografie;
detailed bibliographic data are available in the Internet at http://dnb.ddb.de.

For more information please check: www.die-gestalten.de

Respect copyright, encourage creativity!

✦ ✦

WE WOULD LIKE TO THANK ALL THE DESIGNERS AND ARTISTS FOR THEIR CONTRIBUTION.
WE WOULD LIKE TO THANK THE FOLLOWING PEOPLE FROM MTV FOR THEIR HELP AND GREAT
SUPPORT IN THE MAKING OF THIS BOOK: BRENT HANSEN, CRISTIÁN JOFRÉ, ROB 'HERO' SYKES,
ROB HOOPER, ALEJANDRO ABRAMOVICH, ANDREW LO, BILL ROEDY, CAM LEVIN, CAROLINE
ANSELL, CHARMAINE CHOO, CYRUS OSHIDAR, GEORGIA COOKE, HENRIK WERDELIN, HOLLY
STEVENS, IVAN BOGDANOV, JASON HIRSCHHORN, JEFFREY KEYTON, JOAQUIM RIBES, JUDY
MCGRATH, KEVIN MACKALL, LARS BECKUNG, MARKUS 'MACKY' DRESE, MAUREEN FORDE,
MAURICE HOLS, MAURIZIO VITALE, MIYAKO HATTORI, PETER MOLLER, POLLY STEVENS,
REBECCA JEFFRIES, RODRIGO PIMENTA, TANJA FLINTOFF, THOMAS SABEL, TONY ELISON

✦ ✦